THE DELEGATE FROM NEW YORK

or

PROCEEDINGS OF THE
FEDERAL CONVENTION OF 1787

from the Notes of JOHN LANSING, JR.

John Lansing Jun

THE DELEGATE FROM NEW YORK

or

PROCEEDINGS OF THE FEDERAL CONVENTION OF 1787

from the Notes of
JOHN LANSING, JR.

ༀ

Edited by JOSEPH REESE STRAYER

KENNIKAT PRESS, INC./PORT WASHINGTON, N. Y.

To the Memory of
JOHN LANSING LIVINGSTON
Who Discovered and Preserved
This Manuscript

PREFACE

THE editor of a newly discovered manuscript owes an especial debt of gratitude to the friends who made the discovery and publication possible. My wife, who first heard of the existence of Lansing's notes and suggested that I investigate them, is primarily responsible for bringing this record to light. The owners of the manuscript, Miss Clarisse Livingston and Mrs. Blake Lancaster, very generously permitted the publication of this important document and deserve the thanks of all students of American institutions. Miss Livingston also gave me some valuable information regarding Lansing's life and the history of the notes after his death, while Mrs. Lancaster supplied me with the Lansing family Bible so that I could compare the notes with other specimens of the Chancellor's handwriting.

The Princeton University Library kindly made photostats of the note-books for me. Professor E. S. Corwin of Princeton and Dr. Max Farrand, director of the Huntington Library, were good enough to look over my work in manuscript and to make some very helpful suggestions. Mr. E. Wilder Spaulding of the Department of State assisted me in trying to solve the problems connected with the publication of Yates' notes. Last of all, because he has been interested in the work from beginning to end, I must mention my colleague, Professor T. J. Wertenbaker, who en-

couraged me to undertake the task and who was always ready to help me with the problems which it
raised.

J. R. S.

CONTENTS

INTRODUCTION

WHEN Farrand published his monumental edition of the records of the Federal Convention,[1] he recognized the fact that "it is possible, indeed probable, that other records of the Convention will be brought to light."[2] Most of the men at Philadelphia must have kept some sort of record or memorandum of what was going on in Convention, for their own convenience. Moreover, Gouverneur Morris once remarked that many of his fellow-delegates had "passed their evenings in transcribing speeches from shorthand minutes of the day."[3] Several sets of notes, known to have existed in the years immediately following the Convention, have since disappeared.[4] Thus it is not surprising that a record of the proceedings of the Convention, hitherto unknown to historians, should have been discovered.

This new source consists of a set of notes taken by John Lansing, Jr., one of the three delegates from New York.[5] Although it would seem that the immediate family of the statesman must have known that he had taken notes on the Convention of 1787, his later descendants were not aware of the existence

[1] Max Farrand, *The Records of the Federal Convention of 1787*, 3 v. New Haven, 1911. Cited hereafter as Farrand.

[2] Farrand, I, XXIII.

[3] *ibid.*, III, 419.

[4] *ibid.*, I, XXIII.

[5] There is no doubt that the notes are in Lansing's handwriting. I have compared them with his entries in the Lansing family Bible in the possession of his descendants, and the hands are unquestionably the same.

of these papers until about thirty-five years ago. At that time Lansing's grandson, the late John Lansing Livingston, found the two note-books which contained a record of the proceedings of the Convention in the library of John Lansing Sutherland, another grandson of John Lansing, Jr., and a cousin of Mr. Livingston's. Mr. Sutherland had died in the autumn of 1901, leaving no descendants, and upon the discovery of the notes, Mrs. Sutherland gave them to John Lansing Livingston. Mr. Livingston realized the importance of the documents and earnestly desired to edit and publish them himself. Unfortunately, as he was nearly seventy-two years of age at that time and suffering from ill health, he died, January 9, 1904, before accomplishing his purpose. At the death of John Lansing Livingston, who was a bachelor, the manuscripts came into the possession of his nephew, Edward Livingston, and niece, Clarisse H. Livingston. Since the death of Edward Livingston on November 21, 1929, they have belonged to his wife, the former Mrs. Edward Livingston, now Mrs. Blake Lancaster, and Clarisse H. Livingston, of Manatee, Florida.[6]

John Lansing, Jr., the author of these notes, was born in Albany in 1754.[7] He studied law under Robert Yates and James Duane, and was admitted to practice at Albany in 1775. He served as General Schuyler's military secretary in 1776-77. He soon became engaged in politics, perhaps because of

[6] Miss Clarisse Livingston kindly gave me the account of the history of the manuscript contained in the preceding paragraph.

[7] For Lansing's life, see Robert E. Cushman's account in the *Dictionary of American Biography,* X, 609-10, and the sources there quoted.

his associations with his old master, Yates, who was a rather prominent member of the group which ran the state government. In addition to the support of Yates, Lansing seems also to have had the confidence of the Clintons, who dominated New York during most of his career. He held public office almost constantly from 1780 to 1814, and his first important positions were due to appointments by George Clinton. He was a member of the New York Assembly in 1780-84, 1786, and 1788, serving as speaker in the two last years. He was a member of Congress under the Articles of Confederation, in 1784, and 1785. He was appointed mayor of Albany in 1786, and held this office until 1790. In 1786 he served, with Yates, as a commissioner to settle a territorial dispute with Massachusetts. With Yates and Hamilton he was chosen to represent New York at the Federal Convention in 1787. He attended the Convention for little more than a month, arriving June 2 and withdrawing with Yates, as a protest against the centralizing tendencies of the majority, on July 10. He was also a member of the state convention of 1788, where, with Yates, he opposed ratification of the Constitution. In 1790 he became a judge of the New York Supreme Court. Once more this meant close association with Yates, since the latter had been a judge of this court since 1776, and was chief justice from 1790 to 1798. When Yates surrendered his office, Lansing succeeded him as chief justice of the Supreme Court. In 1801 Lansing became Chancellor of the State of New York, and held this position until he was retired for age in 1814. He remained active in the practice of law until his mysterious disappearance in 1829. On December 12 of that year, he left his hotel in New York City in the late afternoon to post a letter on an Albany boat. He was never seen again. Thurlow Weed in later years claimed that he had discovered the secret of Lansing's death. According to Weed, Lansing was murdered because he knew too much about a certain case which involved the interests of an influential and highly placed group of citizens of New York. Weed always refused to give more precise information, and descendants of Lansing who investigated his story were satisfied that it had no basis of fact.[8] The most likely solution of the mystery is that Lansing, who was seventy-five at the time of his disappearance, missed his footing on the dock or the gang-plank in the dim evening light, fell in the river, and was swept out to sea. Another possibility is that he was robbed and murdered on his way to the boat.

Lansing's early career was that of an able, but subordinate member of a powerful political machine. He was promoted from one position to another because he did his work well, and in accordance with the plans of the leaders. As a judge he was somewhat more independent, competent as ever in his work, but less important in developing the judicial system and law of his state than some of his contemporaries. At the same time his appointment to the bench at the comparatively early age of thirty-six deprived him of the opportunity of becoming one of the active leaders in state politics. He never seems to have exercised decisive influence in this field, though his talents as a debater were appreciated. In the Assembly and in the State Convention of 1788

[8] This statement is based on conversations with Mrs. Lancaster.

he was frequently called on to state his party's case, which he did with a good deal of ability and logic.[9] The portrait of Lansing by the Georgia delegate to the Federal Convention, William Pierce, is certainly unfair in this respect: "Mr. Lansing is a practicing Attorney at Albany and Mayor of that Corporation. He has. a hisitation in his speech, that will prevent his being an Orator of any eminence;—his legal knowledge I am told is not extensive, nor his education a good one. He is however a Man of good sense, plain in his manners, and sincere in his friendships."[10]

While Lansing began his career as a loyal follower of the Clinton machine, he later asserted his independence. He was nominated for governor of New York in 1804, by the Jefferson Republicans, and Hamilton urged the Federalists to support him rather than Burr. In spite of these promising prospects, Lansing withdrew his name, because George Clinton had "sought to pledge him to a particular course of conduct in the administration of the government of the state."[11] He later explained that he had been asked to promise that De Witt Clinton could take his place as Chancellor.

More important from the point of view of evaluating the notes is the fact that while Lansing was closely associated with Yates for almost thirty years, the two men did not always agree. For example, in 1789 Yates ran for governor. In spite of his earlier

[9] *The Debates* and *Proceedings* of the *Constitutional Convention of the State of New York* . . . 1788 (Poughkeepsie, 1905), pp. 11, 62, 87, 119, and 136-7.
[10] Farrand, III, 90.
[11] D. S. Alexander, *A Political History of the State of New York* (New York, 1906), I, 136, 152.

opposition to the Constitution, he was supported by Hamilton and the Federalists, because he seemed less violently opposed to the new government than his opponent, Clinton. Lansing, however, remained loyal to his Clinton connections and opposed Yates, who was defeated by a narrow margin.[12] In the Convention itself, as will appear later, Lansing and Yates did not always agree in their votes. Evidence of disagreement with Yates is important in estimating the extent to which Lansing's notes are an independent source.

It seems evident that the notes were written during Lansing's attendance at the Convention, and were not composed, or even revised at a later date. The records of speeches and votes are too accurate and too detailed to have been written from memory, and at the same time they are independent of any other authority which we now possess. They could not have been composed after the Convention by using other accounts of the proceedings, since they contain information which is not to be found in other records. Unlike Madison, Lansing seems to have made no effort to correct or revise his notes in later years, although he had good opportunities for doing so. Yates' notes were in his possession for a while[13] and he lived to see the publication of the official Journal of the Convention in 1819. However, Lansing made little or no use of his notes after 1787. The only possible reference to them which I can find occurred during an argument with Hamilton in 1788. Lansing,

---

[12] Alexander, *op. cit.,* I, 38 *ff.*

[13] Farrand, I, 536, " 'The preceding notes of the late Chief Justice Yates . . . were copied by me, literally, from the original manuscript in his handwriting. . . .' John Lansing, Jun."

in the New York ratifying convention, said that Hamilton had urged at Philadelphia that "state governments ought to be subverted at least so far as to leave them only corporate rights. . . ."[14] Hamilton denied this warmly, and the controversy continued after the convention had ended its work. In a letter written at this time, Lansing said he was enclosing a statement (unfortunately lost) containing his own opinion and that of Yates as to what Hamilton actually said.[15] This statement was probably based on his notes, but might have been written from memory, since not much more than a year had elapsed since Hamilton had made the speech in question.

Yates' notes on the Convention not only were in Lansing's possession for some time, but he made a copy of them, which was eventually published. This raises the question as to why Lansing preferred to have Yates' notes published, rather than his own. Unfortunately, both the original Yates notes and Lansing's copy of them have disappeared. The first edition of Yates' notes gives absolutely no information about the circumstances of publication, not even

[14] Farrand, III, 338. Lansing's statement was substantially true. Madison reports Hamilton as saying "Subordinate authorities . . . would be necessary. There must be district tribunals: corporations for local purposes. But cui bono, the vast and expensive apparatus now appertaining to the States." It is true that Hamilton a little earlier had said that while there would be a great economy in extinguishing state governments "he did not mean . . . to shock the public opinion by proposing such a measure." (Farrand, I, 287.) Lansing's version of this remark in his notes (cf. p. 65) was: "It will not do to propose formal extinction of State Governments—It would shock public Opinion too much.—Some subordinate Jurisdictions—something like limited Corporations. If general Government properly modified it may extinguish State Governments gradually."

[15] *ibid.*, III, 352.

the name of the editor,[16] so we are reduced to hypotheses. It seems to be true that some members of the Convention felt that no delegate should publish his notes, at least during his own lifetime.[17] As Yates died in 1801, the publication of his notes twenty years later would not seem improper. Moreover, during most of his career Lansing was involved

[16] A. B. Street, *Council of Revision of New York* (Albany 1859), p. 172, says that Yates' widow published the notes. As Lansing had been an associate of her husband's she may have asked him to help her, which would be one explanation of the fact that the notes were printed from his copy. Street, however, gives no source for his statement, which is contradicted by another authority, see below, p. 10.

[17] Farrand, III, 368. Hamilton is quoted as saying in 1792: "the deliberations of the convention, which were carried on in private, were *to remain unmolested. . . .* Had they *been afterwards disclosed,* much food would have been afforded to inflammatory declamation." *ibid.,* 426. William Jackson, secretary of the Convention, told J. Q. Adams on November 19, 1818 (when Adams' edition of the Journal was about to appear) that "he had taken extensive minutes of the debates in the Convention, but, at the request of President Washington, had promised that they should never be published during his own life, which he supposed had been a loss to him of many thousand dollars." *ibid.,* 447. Madison, writing to Thomas Ritchie on September 15, 1821 (several years after the publication of the Journal) regarding the publication of his notes said: "In general it had appeared to me that it might be best to let the work be a posthumous one; or at least that its publication should be delayed till the Constitution should be well settled by practice, and till a knowledge of the controversial part of the proceedings of its framers could be turned to no improper account. Delicacy also seemed to require some respect to the rule by which the Convention 'prohibited a promulgation without leave of what was spoken in it'; so long as the policy of that rule could be regarded as in any degree unexpired." *ibid.,* 427. C. Pinckney wrote on December 30, 1818, that "the Veil of secrecy from the Proceedings of the Convention being removed by Congress (by authorizing publication of the Journal) and but very few of the members alive would make disclosures now of the scenes there acted less improper than before."

in New York politics[18] and publication of his own notes might have involved him in useless and politically dangerous controversies. His argument with Hamilton in 1788 had shown him how easy it was to incur accusations that he had reported proceedings inaccurately, and how difficult it was to prove the truth of any statement about what went on in the Convention. Any one of these reasons might have caused Lansing to keep his own notes secret, and permit the publication of those of Yates.

Finally, there is evidence to show that Lansing took no active part in the publication of Yates' record, but, at the most, merely allowed his copy to be used by others. In 1808 Genêt, the former French minister to the United States, published a *Letter to the Electors of President and Vice-President of the United States*.[19] The letter, as Farrand says, "consisted almost entirely of an abstract or extracts from the notes of Yates . . . cleverly pieced together in such a way as to represent Madison as the leader of the national party in the Federal Convention and working for the annihilation of the state governments."[20] This attack on Madison was obviously inspired by the Clintons. De Witt Clinton was very anxious to secure the nomination of George Clinton for the presidency, and did his best to discredit Madison, who was favored by most of the party leaders outside New York. Even after Madison had been nominated by the Republicans, the Clintons continued their opposition, and tried to keep the New York

[18] See above, p. 3, and D. S. Alexander, *A Political History of the State of New York,* I, 38 *ff.,* 129, 131, 136, 152.
[19] Farrand, III, 410 *ff.*
[20] *ibid.,* I, XIV.

electors from voting for the Virginian. They were not completely successful, but they did manage to split the New York vote.[21] It seems possible that the Clintons learned in some way that Lansing, a member of their organization, possessed a copy of the Yates notes, and that they persuaded him to allow Genêt to use them in an atttempt to discredit Madison. Since Lansing at that time was still Chancellor of New York, it may have appeared improper for him, as a high judicial officer, to assume direct responsibility for a rather unfair attack on a candidate for the presidency. Whatever the reason, Genêt had the Yates notes in his possession in 1808, and he may never have returned them. J. C. Hamilton believed that Genêt was responsible for the complete publication of the notes in 1821,[22] and it is noteworthy that Madison, in his somewhat acrid comments on Yates' record, has nothing to say about Lansing's responsibility in allowing his copy to be used.[23]

Lansing openly admits that he made use of Yates' notes while the Convention was in session. Lansing missed the first five days of the Convention, and his record for those days is simply a duplicate of Yates'. On the sixth day (June 2), when Lansing began taking notes for himself, he followed Yates closely in his record of that day's proceedings. His entry for June 5 begins: "Being indisposed I did not attend but Judge Yates gave me the following Account of their Proceedings."[24] This naturally raises the question as to how independent Lansing's

[21] Alexander, *op. cit.,* I, 166 *ff*.
[22] Quoted in Farrand, I, XIV.
[23] Farrand, III, 446, 497, 521.
[24] See below, p. 32.

record is of Yates' on other days. Even though he did not copy Yates directly, he still may have been influenced by him, especially when the close political and professional connections between the two men are remembered.

The possibility of Yates' influence cannot be entirely excluded, yet there is sufficient evidence to establish Lansing as an independent authority. In the first place, he did not always agree with Yates in his political ideas. It will be remembered that he opposed Yates when the latter ran for governor in 1789, and in the Convention Lansing voted against Yates on at least five occasions.[25] It is difficult to detect any difference in the attitude of the two men during the Convention, yet it seems that Lansing was a little less intransigent than Yates.[26] Lansing did make an effort to persuade the Convention to accept

[25] See below, pp. 50, 77, 83, and Farrand, I, 539, where New York's vote is twice recorded as "divided." Since Hamilton had left the Convention by this date (July 5), Yates and Lansing must have voted against each other.

[26] *The Ratification of the Federal Convention by the State of New York,* C. E. Minor (New York, 1921), p. 80. Yates was quoted by a newspaper of 1788 as saying: "There is not a step towards this business that I ever agreed to; nor is there a sentence in it that I will ever agree to. . . ." On the other hand, in the New York State Convention Lansing said that he was "sensible of the defects of the existing Confederation" and, while he disliked the new Constitution, he did not despair "of making important amendments to the system now offered for consideration." His whole conduct during the state convention bears out this statement. Lansing was one of the most active members in suggesting amendments, and he was one of the committee of thirteen which drew up the final list of amendments submitted to the Convention. (cf. *The Debates and Proceedings of the Constitutional Convention of the State of New York,* pp. 12, 62, 65, 68, 87, 90, 119, 136, 137, and Minor, *op. cit.,* p. 118.)

the New Jersey Plan, which, weak as it was, would have strengthened the Confederation. Yates did not even cooperate to this extent, but sat silent and voted against everything which would have decreased the authority of his state. Again, in two votes on July 6, when the great compromise on representation was being worked out, New York's vote is recorded as "divided," which means that Yates and Lansing could not agree on accepting some of the details of the compromise.[27] From what we know of Yates' attitude at this time, it seems likely that he was the one who was opposing the compromise. He had apparently lost all interest in the Convention, since he stopped taking notes after July 5, although he attended meetings through July 10. Lansing was not quite so hopeless about the proceedings, since his record continues through the 9th. However, both men went home after the 10th, long before the Convention came to an end, and they both signed a letter to the governor of New York protesting that the Convention was greatly exceeding its powers.[28]

The two men not only disagreed from time to time in their principles, but they also differed constantly in reporting the details of the proceedings. It is easy to point out place after place where Lansing gives information which is not to be found in Yates.[29] Verbal parallels between the two records are rare after June 2, and are confined to reports of striking statements which made a deep impression on all hearers. Altogether, it is clear that Lansing wrote his record independently of Yates, and that it can

[27] Farrand, I, 539.
[28] *ibid.,* III, 244.
[29] See below, pp. 37, 43, 47, 48, etc.

be considered an original authority. Even where
Lansing avowedly copied Yates, his version does not
agree absolutely with the printed text, which is the
only form in which the latter's notes exist. There
are many verbal differences, some of which are important.[30] For example, the printed text of Yates
fails to specify whether a speech on May 30 was
made by C. Pinckney or C. C. Pinckney, whereas
Lansing's copy ascribes it to the former. On May
31, the printed version has "This day the state of
Jersey was represented," while Lansing correctly sub-
stitutes "Georgia." Granting that Lansing, arriving
late at the Convention and hurriedly copying Yates'
notes, would be apt to make many minor mistakes
in his work, such discrepancies as the above suggest
that the printed version of Yates' notes may be somewhat inaccurate. The first edition of Yates' *Secret
Proceedings* was not based on the original manuscript, but on a copy, and it shows no signs of careful editing. Thus it seems likely that many errors
may exist in the text as we have it.

As for Lansing's technique in composing his own
record, he seems to have been one of the men mentioned by G. Morris "who passed their evenings in
transcribing speeches from shorthand minutes of the
day."[31] There is considerable evidence which indicates
that Lansing took rough notes during the sessions
of the Convention, and later copied them in expanded
form in his note-books.[32] Sometimes he seems to have

[30] See the notes on the first 11 pages of Lansing's text.
[31] Farrand, III, 419.
[32] See below, p. 54. Here Lansing copied a phrase at the
top of a page in his note-book, and then, a little later on, re-
copied, and immediately crossed out, the same phrase. The fact

neglected to copy his notes immediately, and to have written up two days' proceedings at the same time. For example, he failed to make a break between the events of June 11 and June 12, and entered them all under the first date.[33] Later on he recorded the debates of June 16 under the date of June 15, and forgot to make a complete correction.[34] At the end of his entries for June 19, he inserted, and then crossed out, a phrase which he wrote again in its proper place at the beginning of the next day's debate.[35]

In addition to notes on speeches and votes, Lansing copied several important documents of the Convention. The Virginia Plan is entered in the back of his first note-book. Naturally this copy could be made only after he arrived on June 2, and it incorporates in the text changes voted by the Committee of the Whole before that date.[36] Lansing kept his copy of the Plan up to date by inserting and crossing out phrases so that it would conform to the results of successive votes in the Committee of the Whole.[37] He also furnishes a copy of the final report of the Committee of the Whole. This was corrected only once, to show the results of a vote of the Convention on June 20.[38]

Lansing's manuscript gives interesting material about the characters and opinions of members of the

that he occasionally records speeches out of their proper order would also indicate hasty copying of loose notes, see p. 69.

[33] See below, p. 48.
[34] See below, p. 55.
[35] See below, p. 71.
[36] See below p. 113.
[37] See below, p. 115.
[38] See below, p. 109.

Convention, since it records sentences and speeches which are not given by other authorities. Lansing's notes also help to explain some speeches and events which are rather obscure in other records. For example, only in Lansing is the development of Charles Pinckney's plan for the Senate clearly presented.[39] Lansing also reported parts of Hamilton's speeches better than either Madison or Yates. Thus he emphasized Hamilton's important distinction between the ease of coercing individuals, and the difficulty of coercing states,[40] and Hamilton's proof that the large states could not combine to oppress the small, since their commercial interests were so different.[41] Two important constitutional questions that were raised during the Convention are reported by Lansing alone. On June 8, C. Pinckney asked who was to be the arbiter if state and national governments disagreed on the interpretation of the new articles of union.[42] In dealing with the issue of states' rights, James Wilson said that "the Declaration of Independence declares the U. S. collectively to be vested with the Power of making War and Peace—this antecedent to framing (state) Constitutions consequently paremount [sic]."[43] In other words there never were sovereign states because the United States as a collective

[39] See below, p. 57, where Pinckney gives the example of the Lycian League, in which each state had one to three votes; p. 101, where Pinckney proposes to divide the states into classes "to have from one to four votes."

[40] See below, p. 64.

[41] See below, p. 70.

[42] See below, p. 39.

[43] See below, p. 69. King seems to have understood this point. but Madison and Yates missed it.

unit had sovereign powers before state governments were created.

Lansing's explanation of the final vote on the New Jersey Plan is interesting. Though he had been an ardent supporter of the plan, he admitted it had failed to unite the interests of the state-rights group. The New Jersey Plan was open to serious objections, even from the point of view of the enemies of centralization, and it involved too many side issues. Therefore, says Lansing, it was allowed to drop without much protest, and the leaders of the opposition tried to center the debate on the question of representation,[44] the only point on which the antagonists of the Virginia Plan could agree. To insist on an equal number of votes for each state in both Houses was a policy which involved none of the dangers of the New Jersey Plan, and at the same time made it possible to obtain recruits from the other camp. The course of events shows that Lansing's explanation of this shift in tactics is correct. The New Jersey Plan mustered only a few supporters in the final vote on its fate. But, as soon as it was killed, the great debate on the question of representation began, in which the state-rights group was able to gain enough strength to deadlock the Convention.

Lansing's work is valuable in affording opportunity to check the accuracy of Madison and Yates by confronting them with a new authority. Usually their record is confirmed by Lansing. Without using exactly the same words, he gives the same ideas, the same arguments, which are found in the other authorities. Phrases and speeches which are found in

[44] See below, p. 70.

only one record are frequently confirmed by Lansing,[45] thus showing that Madison's failure to report a remark recorded by Yates, or vice versa, is no reason to doubt that the statement was made.

Lansing's notes are also useful in checking the accuracy of some of the many additions and corrections which Madison made to his *Debates* in the years after the Convention. It is well known that in spite of his condemnation of Yates' *Secret Proceedings,* Madison copied into his manuscript many sentences and phrases taken directly from Yates. In most cases Lansing confirms the accuracy of these borrowings.[46] Madison likewise revised some of his notes to make them conform to the record of the official Journal. The Journal was so badly kept that this was a dangerous procedure, but Lansing's authority shows that some, at least, of these revisions were justified.[47] In short, the discovery of Lansing's notes proves that Madison's and Yates' accounts of the proceedings of the Convention are on the whole trustworthy and accurate, and that it is safe to use one to supply the deficiencies of the other. This is of importance, considering that the original of Yates' *Proceedings* has disappeared, and that Madison made so many additions and corrections to his *Debates* in the half-

[45] e.g., pp. 40, 42, 46 confirms remarks in Yates, omitted by Madison. On pp. 41, 92, 98 he confirms remarks in Madison, omitted by Yates.

[46] pp. 46, 82, 94, 97, 99. However, Madison was misled by Yates at least once. Copying Yates, he states that the plan to retire one-third of the Senate every two years was accepted on June 25, whereas it seems certain from other sources that the vote on this resolution came on June 26. In this case, Lansing disagrees with Yates and Madison, but agrees with the Journal.

[47] See below, pp. 51, 82, 87, 92.

century following the Convention that they lost some of their value as a strictly contemporary record.

However, while the records of Madison and Yates are, on the whole, accurate, it is possible to see, in the light of Lansing's notes, that they are incomplete. Each writer had a tendency to suppress indiscrete and irritating remarks made by members of his own party, and to stress such remarks when made by the opposition. The partisans of centralization could not always resist the temptation to point to horrible examples of misrule and anarchy in some of the states as an argument for strengthening the national government. Such remarks could easily be turned against them in debate, and were useful in stirring up local patriotism against the Constitution. It is easy to see that Madison would be anxious to forget such irritating episodes and would fail to mention them in his notes. For example, he failed to record two attacks on the government of Rhode Island,[48] and crossed out of his notes on one of his own speeches a remark deprecating Georgia's war with the Indians.[49] On the other hand, Lansing and Yates were careful to record such remarks, as well as threats by representatives of large states that they would use force or commercial pressure against the small states rather than accept the principle of equal representation in Congress.[50] Like Madison, the two New York delegates tried to smooth over the indiscretions of members of their group, notably the remarks of Bedford, in which he suggested that the small states would seek

[48] See below, pp. 57, 73.

[49] See below, p. 68. Yates, Lansing, and King all agree that Madison made this remark.

[50] See below, pp. 93, 104.

help from abroad if the large states insisted on the Virginia Plan.[51] Madison, of course, reported this incident fully.

Lansing's notes cover only the first period of the Convention, during which interest was concentrated on the question of representation. As Lansing says, this was the one point on which the opposition could unite. Everyone agreed that the federal government needed more power; the real issue was over the control of this power. There was comparatively little protest against increasing the authority of the central government, but there were innumerable speeches denouncing the idea of representation in direct proportion to population. As one of the delegates remarked, if the small states had been assured an equal share of the power, they would very likely have accepted the plan of the Committee of the Whole.[52] What they feared was less a strong national government than a government dominated by Virginia, Pennsylvania, and Massachusetts.

Lansing's notes throw new light on these state jealousies, and this is their chief value for the general historian. Since he left the Convention before the Constitution was put into its final form his record does not often give precise information about specific clauses. But as a new source from which we can recreate the atmosphere of the Convention and estimate the character of the leading delegates it has great importance.

[51] See below, pp. 100, 102, 104.
[52] See below, p. 57.

PROCEEDINGS OF THE CONVENTION, VOL. I*

MAY 25, 1787

p. 1　　Attended the Convention of the States[1] at the State House in Philadelphia when the following States were represented.[2]

> New York—by Col. Hamilton and myself.
>
> Iersey—by Iudge Brearsley, Mr. Houston, and Mr. Paterson.
>
> Pennsylvania—by Robert Morris, Iames Wilson, G. Morris, Mr. Fitzsimmons.
>
> Deleware—Iudge Reed, Mr. Broome, and Mr. Basset.
>
> Virginia—General Washington, Governor Randolph, Mr. Wyth, Mr. Mason, Mr. Matthewson.
>
> North Carolina—
>
> South Carolina—Mr. Rutlege, C. Pinkney, C. C. Pinkney, Mr. Butler.

p. 2　　A Motion by R. Morris[3] that General Washington take the Chair unanimously agreed to.

* Throughout the footnotes M. refers to Madison's account of the day's proceedings and Y. to Yates'; both as printed by Farrand.

[1] L. did not attend the Convention until June 2. His account of the proceedings to that date is copied from Yates. Variants from the printed version of Yates are given in footnotes.

[2] Rufus King of Massachusetts, John Blair and James McClurg of Virginia, Alexander Martin, William Davie, Richard Spaight and Hugh Williamson of North Carolina, and Few of Georgia are listed in the Journal as present. The printed version of Yates gives the delegates from North Carolina; otherwise it is the same as this.

[3] Y. inserts "and seconded".

When seated he[4] declared that as he never had been in a similar Situation[5] he felt himself embarrassed—that he hoped his Errors as they were[6] unintentional would be excused.

Mr. Hamilton in behalf of the State of New York moved that Major Iackson be appointed Secretary—The Delegates from[7] Pennsylvania moved for Temple Franklin—Carried for Iackson[8] who was[9] called in and took his Seat.

After which the respective Credentials of the seven States were read—N.B. That of Deleware restrained its Delegates from assenting to an Abolition of the 5*th* Section[10] of the Confederation which directed[11] that each State shall have a vote.[12]

p. 3

Door-keepers and Messengers being appointed the House adjourned to Monday the 28*th* Day of May at 10 o'Clock.

Monday, May 28th

Met pursuant to Adjourement. A Committee of three Members (whose Appointment I omitted in the Entry of the Proceedings on Friday last)[13] reported a Set of Rules for the Order of the Convention which being considered by Articles were agreed to and additional ones proposed and referred to the

[4] Y. inserts "(Gen. Washington)".
[5] Y. "such a situation".
[6] Y. "would be".
[7] Y. "for".
[8] Y. "by a majority Mr. Jackson carried it".
[9] Y. "who was" omitted.
[10] Y. "article".
[11] Y. "by which it is declared".
[12] Y. "one".
[13] M. This committee consisted of Wythe, Hamilton, and C. Pinckney.

same Committee. The Representation was this Day encreased to nine States—Massachusetts and Connecticut became[14] represented.

Adjourned to next Day.

p. 4   TUESDAY

Met pursuant to Adjournm't.[15]
The additional Rules agreed to.

His Excellency Governor Randolph, a Member from Virginia,[16] in a long and elaborate Speech shewed the Defects in the System of the present foederal Government as totally inadequate to the Peace, Safety and Security of the Confederation and the absolute Necessity of a more energetic Government. He closed his[17] Remarks with a Set of Resolutions[18] which he proposed to the Convention for their Adoption and as leading Principles whereon to form a new Government—he candidly confessed that they were not intended for a foederal Government— he meant a strong, *consolidated* Union in which the p. 5 Idea of States should be nearly annihilated—(Copy of these Resolutions is marked a.)[19]

He then moved that they should be taken up in a[20] Committee of the whole House.

Mr. C. Pinkney, a Member from South Carolina[21] added that he had reduced his Ideas of a new

[14] Y. "becoming".
[15] Y. omits this phrase.
[16] Y. inserts "got up, and".
[17] Y. "these".
[18] Y. inserts "fifteen in number".
[19] Y. "I have taken a copy of these resolutions, which are hereto annexed". L.'s copy of the resolutions is below, p. 113.
[20] Y. omits "a".
[21] Y. inserts "then".

Government to a System which he read and confessed that it was grounded on Principles similar to those in the Resolutions.[22]

The House then resolved that they would[23] next Day form themselves into a Committee of the whole to take into Consideration the State of the Union.

Adjourned to next Day.

WEDNESDAY, 30TH MAY

Met[24] pursuant to adjournm't.

p. 6 The Convention pursuant to order resolved itself into a Committee of the whole.

Mr. Gorham (a member of[25] Massachusetts) appointed Chairman.

Mr. Randolph then moved his *first Resolution*[26]—b.[27]

Mr. G. Morris observed that it was an unnecessary Resolution as the subsequent Resolutions would not square with it.

It was then withdrawn by the Proposer and in Lieu thereof the following were proposed—here Resolutions Q.[28]

[22] Y. "on the same principle as of the above Resolutions."

[23] Y. inserts "the".

[24] Y. "Convention met".

[25] Y. "from".

[26] Y. "resolve, to wit:".

[27] Copied by L. in the back of his note-book and marked "b". It reads "Resolved that the Articles of Confederation ought to be so corrected and enlarged as to accomplish the Objects proposed by their Institution namely common Defence Security of Liberty and general Welfare".

[28] These resolutions, copied by Lansing (below, p. 118), read: "1. Resolved—That a Union of the States merely foederal will not accomplish the Objects proposed by the Articles of Confederation namely—Common Defence, Security of Liberty, and General Welfare. 2d. Resolved—That no Treaty or Treaties

In considering the Question on the first Resolve various Modifications were proposed when Mr. C.[29] Pinkney observed at last that if the Convention agreed to it it appeared to him the[30] Business was at p. 7 an End for as the Powers of the House in general were to revise the present Confederation and to alter and[31] amend it as the Case might require, and[32] to determine its Inefficacy[33] or Incapability of Amendment or Improvement must End in a[34] Dissolution of the Powers.

This Remark had its Weight and in Consequence of it the 1st and 2nd Resolve was droped and the Question agitated on the third.

This last resolve had also its Difficulties—the Term *Supreme* required Explanation—it was asked whether it was intended to annihilate State Governments.[35] It was answered[36] only so far as the Powers intended to be granted to the new Government should

among any of the States as Sovereign will accomplish or secure their common Defence Liberty or Welfare. 3rdly. Resolved that a national Government ought to be established consisting of a supreme judicial Legislature and executive."

This agrees with M. and Y. except for some very slight verbal differences, e.g. M. and Y. have "legislative" in the third resolution.

[29] Y. omits "C". McHenry ascribes this remark (in a weaker form) to C. C. Pinckney. M. merely notes that the discussion of the first resolution was postponed because of "verbal criticisms".

[30] Y. "that their".

[31] Y. "or".

[32] Y. omits "and".

[33] Y. "insufficiency".

[34] Y. "the".

[35] According to M. this question was raised by C. Pinckney.

[36] Mc Henry ascribes this remark to Randolph.

clash with the States,[37] the latter was to yield. The[38] Question was then put—

p. 8

for the Resolve	Against it
Massachusetts	Connecticut
Pennsylvania	New York—divided
Deleware	[39]The other States unrepresented
Virginia	
North Carolina	
South Carolina	

The next Question was on the following Resolve—[40]

In Substance, that the Mode of the present Representation in Congress[41] was unjust—the Suffrage ought to be in Proportion of[42] Numbers or Property.[43]

To this Deleware objected in Consequence of the Instructions[44] in their Credentials and moved for postponing it which was agreed to.[45] Adjourned till to Morrow.

[37] Y. inserts "when".

[38] Y. omits this phrase.

[39] Y. "Jersey and".

[40] Y. "resolution".

[41] Y. omits "in Congress".

[42] Y. "to".

[43] This is Randolph's second resolution "that the rights of suffrage in the national Legislature ought to be proportioned to the Quotas of Contribution or to the Number of free Inhabitants as the one or other Rule may seem best in different Cases."

[44] Y. "restrictions".

[45] Y. "to have the consideration thereof postponed to which the house agreed".

Thursday, May 31st

Met pursuant to Adjournment.

p. 9   This Day the State of Georgia[46] was represented[47] so that there were now ten States represented.

The House[48] again in[49] a Committee of the whole.[50]

The third Resolve[51] "that the national Legislature ought to consist of two Branches" was taken into Consideration and without any Debate agreed to.[52]

The 4th Resolve "that the Members of the first Branch of the national Legislature ought to be elected by the People of the several States" was opposed[53] by Massachusetts and Connecticut who supposed they ought to be elected[54] by the Legislature[55] and Virginia supported the Resolve, alledging that this ought to be the democratic Branch[56] and as such immediately vested in the People.[57]

---

[46] Y. "Jersey". From the Journal it appears that L.'s version is correct.

[47] Y. "in convention".

[48] Y. inserts "went".

[49] Y. "into".

[50] Y. adds "Mr. Gorham in the chair".

[51] Y. inserts "to wit".

[52] L. omitted Y.'s explanation that he "could not see any objection to its being in two branches". According to M., Pennsylvania opposed this resolution. Farrand thinks that M. was probably wrong in making this statement.

[53] Y. inserts "and strange to tell".

[54] Y. "chosen".

[55] Y. "legislatures".

[56] Y. inserts "of government".

[57] According to M., Sherman of Connecticut and Gerry of Massachusetts opposed election by the people, while Mason and Madison of Virginia and Wilson of Pennsylvania were for it.

p. 10   The[58] Question was carried but the remaining Part of the Resolve detailing the Powers was postponed.

The 5*th* Resolve[59]—postponed.

The 6*th* Resolved detailed—[60].

That each Branch ought to possess the Right of originating Acts. Agreed.

That the National Legislature ought to be empowered to enjoy the Legislative Rights vested in Congress by the Confederation. *Agreed.*

[61]to legislate in all Cases in[62] which[63] seperate States are incompetent. *Agreed.*

Adjourned.[64]

FRIDAY, IUNE 1ST

Met pursuant to Adjournm't.

[65]7*th* Resolve. That a national Executive be instituted. *Agreed.*

to continue in Office[66] 7 Years. *Agreed.*

p. 11   a general Authority to execute the Laws. *Agreed.*

to appoint all Officers not otherwise provided for. Agreed.

[58] Y. "This".

[59] Y. "That the members of the second branch of the national legislature ought to be elected by those of the first out of a proper number of persons nominated by the individual legislatures, and the detail of the mode of election and duration of office was postponed".

[60] Y. "is taken in detail".

[61] Y. "And, moreover".

[62] Y. "to".

[63] Y. inserts "the".

[64] Omitted by Y.

[65] Y. inserts "The".

[66] Y. inserts "for".

Adjourned to[67] next Day.[68]

Thus far Iudge Yates—I having been prevented from attending the Convention at an earlier Day.

SATURDAY, IUNE 2D

Attended Convention.[69]

Present eleven States.

Mr. Pinkney called for the Order of the Day— Resolved into a Committee of the whole.

Mr. Wilson moved that the States should be divided into Districts consisting of one or more States and each District to elect a Number of Senators to form the second Branch of the national Legislature—the Senators to be elected and a certain Proportion to be annually dismissed—avowedly on the Plan of the *New York Senate*.[70]

p. 12

Question put—rejected.

In the *7th* Resolve the words *to be chosen by the national Legislature* agreed to.

President Franklin moved that the Consideration of that Part of the *7th* Resolve which had in Object the making Provision for a Compensation for the Service of the executive be postponed for the Purpose of considering a Motion that the *Executive should receive no Salary Stipend or Emolument for*

[67] Y. inserts "the".

[68] This very brief account of the proceedings on June 1 gives a deceptive appearance of unanimity among the members of the Convention. M.'s notes show that there was prolonged debate on every article adopted.

[69] Lansing followed Yates closely in his account of this day's proceedings. There are only slight verbal differences between the two reports.

[70] As Farrand points out, Yates (and Lansing) misunderstood Wilson's proposal. Wilson wanted to have presidential electors, not senators, chosen in this manner.

the Devotion of his Time to the public Services but that its[71] Expences should be paid.

Postponed Consideration.

Mr. Dickenson moved that in the 7th Resolve[72]

p. 13 the words *and removeable on Impeachment and Conviction for malconduct or Neglect in the Execution of the Duties of the Office*[73] should be inserted after the words *ineligible a second Time.* Agreed.

The Remainder postponed.

Mr. Butler moved to fix the Number of which the Executive should consist.[74] Ent(ere)d on Consideration.

Mr. Randolph—Sentiments of the People ought to be consulted—they will not bear the Semblance of Monarchy—he prefered three Divisions of the States and one Executive to be taken from each—this Division obvious—it had been marked for other Purposes—If a single Executive Persons remote from him neglected—Local Views would be attrib-

p. 14 uted to him, frequently well founded—often without Reason—this would excite Disatisfaction—he was therefore for an *Executive of three.*[75]

[71] L. first wrote "their", crossed it out, and substituted "its".

[72] L. first wrote "after" in this place, and then crossed it out.

[73] This is a garbled account of the proceedings. M. and the Journal agree that Dickinson's motion was that the executive was "to be removeable by the national legislature upon request by a majority of the legislatures of the individual states". This was lost. Then the clause "ineligible a second time" was passed, and then on Williamson's motion the words "and to be removeable on impeachment and conviction of mal-practice or neglect of duty" were added.

[74] Neither the Journal nor M. mention this motion.

[75] M. omitted all references to the triple executive and division of the country in his original account of the speech; he later added a short sentence on the proposition, probably taken, as Farrand thinks, from Yates.

Butler—Delays, Divisions, and Dissentions arise from an Executive consisting of many—Instance Holland distracted State occasioned by her many Councellors.

further Consideration postponed.

Mr. C. Pinkney—Notice for Reconsideration of Mode of Election of the first Branch of the Legislature.[76]

Adjourned till Monday next.

MONDAY, IUNE 4TH[77]

Mr. Pinkney moved that the Blank in the *7th* Resolution fixing the Number of the Executive be p. 15 filled with the Word *one*.[78]

Mr. Wilson—It is congenial to the Feelings of the People to have a single Executive—they have been accustomed to it—Every State has a single Person as Executive—three may divide and adopt distinct Propositions.

Mr. Sherman—ought to have a single Executive but a Council to aid him.

Question whether Blank shall be filled with the Word *one*.

Affirm.		Neg.	
Massachusetts	1	New York	1
Connecticut	1	Deleware	1
Pennsylvania	1	Maryland	1
Virginia	1		—
North Carolina	1		3
South Carolina	1		
Georgia	1		
	7		

[76] This notice is not recorded in any other account (except Y.).

[77] From this point on, L.'s notes are independent of Yates', except for the proceedings of June 5, when L. was ill.

[78] This motion had been made on June 2 (M. and Journal) but was postponed.

The 8*th* Clause was then considered.—Mr.
p. 16 Gerry moved its Postponement to take up the following "that a national Executive shall have a Right
to negative every national Act *which shall not be
afterward past unless by—Part of each Branch of
the national Legislature.*"

Mr. Wilson and Mr. King spoke in its Favor.

Question carried for postponing *6 Ayes—4
Noes.*

Next Question on Motion by Mr. Wilson that
the Executive have an uncontroulled Negative by
expunging the Words scored. Dr. Franklin—Mr.
Maddison and Mr. Bedford against expunging.

Carried unanimously against it.

Motion by Mr. Butler that the Executive be
p. 17 vested with a Power to suspend all Act of national
Legislature for   Days.

Unanimously carried in the Negative.[79]

9*th* Resolve—that a national Iudiciary be established. Agreed *8 States to 2*—Connecticut and Maryland negative.[80]

Adjourned till to Morrow.

IUNE 5TH

Met pursuant to Adjournment.

Being indisposed I did not attend but Iudge

[79] L. omits here the fact that after this vote the Committee of
the Whole agreed to give the executive a veto which could be
overridden by two-thirds of each branch of the legislature.

[80] According to M. there was no opposition to this proposal.
It seems probable that L. confused this vote with the vote on
the question of the veto power, (which he forgot to record in
its proper place) since, according to M. and the Journal, the
resolution granting the veto power passed 8 to 2, with Connecticut and Maryland in the negative.

Yates gave me the following Account of their Proceedings.[81]

The 9th Resolve. *That a national Iudicial be established to consist of one Supreme Tribunal and of Inferior Tribunals*—agreed to—unanimously.[82]

Mr. Wilson moved that the Iudicial be appointed p. 18 by the Executive instead of *the national Legislature.* Mr. Maddison opposed—the Iudges ought to be appointed by the Senetorial Branch of the Legislature. Moves *that* the words *the national Legislature* be struck out.

Carried 8 for and 2 against it.[83]

Good Behaviour and fixed Salaries carried unanimously.

The Remainder of the Clause postponed.

10. Resolve[84]—Read and agreed to.

11. Resolve[85]—Read and postponed.

12. Resolve[86]—Read and agreed to.

13. Resolve[87]—Read and postponed.

---

[81] This account follows the printed version of Y. but is more condensed. It looks as if Y. gave L. his rough notes and that when Y. later copied these notes into his own journal he filled in ellipses and touched up the style.

[82] Y. makes this vote cover the provisions for holding office during good behavior and for fixed salaries. The Journal and M. show that L. was right in stating that these clauses were agreed to separately later in the proceedings.

[83] The Journal agrees with this record, but M. gives 9 ayes and 2 noes.

[84] Providing for the admission of new states.

[85] Guaranteeing republican government and territorial integrity to the states.

[86] Continuing the old Congress to a fixed date and giving assurance that the obligations of Congress would be fulfilled.

[87] Stating that provision should be made for amending the new system without requiring assent of the national legislature.

14. Resolve[88]—Same.

15. Resolve[89]—Mr. Maddison enforced the Necessity of this Resolve for that the new Constitution ought to have the highest Source of Authority —at least paramount to the several Constitutions— p. 19 points out the Mischiefs arising from the present Confederation depending on ordinary State Authorities—Instance the Effect of Treaties when contrasted with antecedent Acts of Legislature.

Mr. King—the People have tacitly agreed to the Confederation and that the Legislature[90] have a Right to confirm any Alterations in it. A Convention of the States[91] however the most eligible to confirm new Government.

Mr. Wilson—People must ratify—all will not come in soon—but as the States do they will confederate.[92]

Postponed 7 States to 3.

[88] Requiring an oath from state officials to support the national government.

[89] Y. "That the amendment which shall be offered to the confederation, ought at a proper time or times after the approbation of congress to be submitted to an assembly or assemblies of representatives, recommended by the several legislatures, to be expressly chosen by the people, to consider and decide thereon."

[90] Y. inserts "in every state".

[91] Y. "a convention in each state". M. is not clear on this point. He has King say "A Convention being a single house, the adoption may more easily be carried thro' it than thro' the Legislatures where there are several branches." This might refer to one convention for all the states, or to a convention in each state.

[92] This is a very condensed version of Y., who has "Mr. Wilson is of opinion, that the people by a convention are the only power that can ratify the proposed system of the new government. It is possible that not all the states, nay, that not even a majority, will immediately come into the measure; but such as do ratify it will be immediately bound by it, and others as they may from time to time accede to it."

Question on 9*th* Resolve to strike out *Inferior Tribunals*.[93] Carried by 5 States against 4. 2 States divided—New York of that Number.

p. 20   Mr. Wilson—in Addition to this Clause—*that the National Legislature shall have the Authority to appoint Inferior Tribunals*. Carried 7 States against 3[94]—New York divided.

Adjourned till to Morrow.

IUNE 6TH

Met according to Adjournment.

4*th* Resolve—C. Pinkney moves—dele *People* and insert *Legislature*.[95]

Messrs. Wilson, Gerry, Sherman spoke in Favor of Amendment. Mr. Mason, Mr. Reed, Mr. Dickinson and Mr. Maddison against it.[96]

Mr. Sherman in the Course of his Remarks observed that the general Government could only have the Regulation of Trade and some other matters of general Concern and not to all the Affairs of the Union.

p. 21   Wilson moved to reconsider that Part of the System which gives the Executive a Right of objecting to *national Laws* and to *Iudicial as a Council of Revision*.[97]

[93] This motion was made by Rutledge.

[94] Madison records the vote as 8 to 2, but the Journal agrees with L. and Y.

[95] This would have meant that the lower house would be chosen by the state legislatures.

[96] This very important debate, which L. records in such a summary way, really turned on the question as to whether the national government was to derive its power from the people or from the states. The motion was lost.

[97] Wilson's motion was to the effect that the veto power should be exercised by the executive "with a convenient number of the national Judiciary."

Mr. Maddison seconded it.

Neg. 8 States—Affirm. 3. New York aff.

C. Pinkney gave Notice that on Friday[98] he would move to reconsider the Clause authorizing national Legislature to negative all Laws.[99]

Adjourned till to Morrow.

IUNE 7TH

Met according to Adjourm't.

5*th* Resolution considered.

C. Pinkney—the Number of which the second p. 22 Branch was to consist ought previously to be fixed. If each of the smaller States is to have one will amount at least to *86*.[100]

Dickenson—Supposed Legislatures ought to elect—he was for House of Peers or something similar. He moved the following Resolve—

Resolved that the Members of the second Branch of the national Legislature ought to be elected by the Individual Legislatures.

Mr. Williamson moved that after Legislature the Words *consisting of* . . . . should be inserted. Supposes *100* Senators would be agreed to—he would be content to reduce them to *25*.

Mr. Wilson—As Convention have already voted a national Government foederal Principles cannot p. 23 obtain. If so, we ought to try to procure different Views and different Sentiments—Representation cannot be proportioned by Numbers—Propagation

[98] The Journal has "tomorrow", that is, Thursday. However, it goes on to say that Friday was selected as the day on which the motion was to be discussed.

[99] That is, all *state* laws.

[100] M. "80".

by best Calculation so rapid as to double Number of Inhabitants every 25 Years—Of Consequence if Representation encreased in proportion to Population the older the Government the weaker and more debilitated would it be. He proposed a Division into Districts for Representation—that Division to be permanent.[101]

Mr. Ianifer—Representation ought to be proportioned by Contribution.[102]

p. 24   Mr. Mason—Can Gentlemen suppose that so extended an Empire can be benefited in proportion to the Burthens to which they submit to support it.—Is not for annihilating Individual States—a large Majority of the Legislature on most local Questions cannot be properly informed of those Circumstances which perhaps are indispensibly necessary to enable them to form a Iudgment.[103]

[101] The reports of this speech differ widely. M.'s version stresses the fact that Wilson was opposed to election of the Senate by the legislatures and wanted the Senate to be chosen by the people. Y. emphasizes the fact that Wilson wanted to preserve strong state governments, although he admits that Wilson wanted the national government to be independent of the State governments. King's version agrees with M. None of them mention the argument reported by L., that population was growing too rapidly to apportion representation by numbers and that the number of Senators assigned to each district should be permanent.

[102] This remark is not recorded by other authorities.

[103] M., Y., and King agree that this speech was made after Wilson's motion had been defeated. L.'s version omits the argument stressed in King's report, that the national government with power of vetoing state laws is already too strong, but he includes a point reported by no one else, namely that the national legislature would be uninformed about local conditions. L. also omitted the conclusion of Mason's speech, which was that the Senate should be chosen by the state legislatures.

Maddison—If each State retained its Sovereignty an Equality of Suffrage would be proper, but not so now.[104]

Dickenson—National Government like the Sun the Centre of the planetary System should rule attract pervade and brighten all the States—but cannot abolish State Governments.[105]

p. 25   Wilson—Does not wish to extinguish State Governments—but believes they will neither warm or brighten the Sun—Rome in her most powerful Imperial State could not effectually pervade and protect every Part of its Dominion nor could the U.S.[106]

Moved by Mr. Wilson—*that the second Branch be elected by the People of certain Districts to be formed for that Purpose.* And that the Resolution be postponed.

Mr. Maddison same Opinion.

Question put. *Negatived.*

Question on original Clause as moved by Dickenson.

[104] This is not a very fair or adequate account of M.'s speech. According to his own version (and King's) he stated briefly that equal representation in the Senate was "unjust" and then passed to his main point, which was that the number of Senators must be kept down. The fact that L. recorded the one sentence which might be construed as an attack on the states, and omitted the body of the argument dealing with the nature and functions of the senate is significant.

[105] Dickinson was arguing for the theory of checks and balances. King has him say "let the General Government be the Sun and the States the Planets repelled yet attracted, and the whole moving regularly and harmoniously in their respective orbits." He accused Wilson of wishing to destroy the states.

[106] L., like Y., records the statements of Wilson which are favorable to state governments and omits his remark (reported by M. and King) that he was afraid that the states might destroy the national government.

Carried unanimously.

Adjourned till to Morrow.

p. 26   IUNE 8TH

Met according to Adjournm't.

Motion by·Mr. C. Pinkney to reconsider 6th[107] Resolve to substitute instead of the Words *contravening in the Opinion of the national Legislature the Articles of the Union* the Words *which shall appear improper.*

Maddison, C. Pinkney and Dickenson spoke in Favor of it—Williamson, Bedford and Sherman against it.

Question—Massachusetts, Virginia, and Pennsylvania for it, one divided[108] and other 7 States against it.

C. Pinkney—on the above Subject. Indispensibly necessary to vest a great controuling Power in national Legislature, which may like the Centre of the plenetary System retain all the sur-

p. 27 rounding Planets in their proper Orbits—the Individual States must submit to this Controul for the general Benefit. The Power as expressed in the Resolution must be productive of Contention and if a Difference in Sentiment arises who is to be the Arbiter?[109]

---

[107] This motion refers to the 6th resolution, which gave the national legislature power to veto state laws "contravening . . . the Articles of Union."

[108] Delaware.

[109] This version of Pinckney's speech differs somewhat from that in other authorities, notably in raising the question as to what authority would have the final power of interpreting the Constitution.

Williamson—The national Legislature ought not to have a Right to negative any Laws but such as may operate to the Prejudice of the Nation.

Madison—wished the precise Line of Power could be ascertained—But totally impracticable—for if a Dispute arises the State Iudiciaries are compelled to expound the Laws so as to give those of the individual State an Operation—National Government *centrifugal*.[110]

p. 28   Gerry—Is doubtful whether it is the Intention of Gentle(men) to give this Power a retrospective Effect—wishes it explained—has no Objection (among others) to extend it to Emission of paper Money.[111]

C. Pinkney—If this acceded to it will operate to abrogate all State Laws and even Constitutions incompatible with national Government.[112]

Wilson—National Government implies the Idea

---

[110] L. follows Y. rather closely in reporting this speech. In M.'s own report of the speech, there is no reference to decisions of state judges. M. felt that the complete veto power was necessary because the national government could not use force against unconstitutional acts of the states. L. misunderstood the last phrase of the speech; M. said that the national government "must controul the centrifugal tendency of the states."

[111] M., Y., and King give accounts of this speech which indicate that Gerry was much more strongly opposed to the motion than could be gathered from L.'s version. Gerry was willing to grant the veto power only in certain specified cases, such as emission of paper money.

[112] M. and King did not report this speech. Y.'s version is a little more definite; it runs "the proposed amendment hàd no retrospect to the state laws already made. The adoption of the new government must operate as a complete repeal of all the constitutions and state laws, as far as they are inconsistent with the new government."

of an Absorbtion of State Sovereignty.[113] Congress in compliance with Wishes of Individual States and from an accomodating Disposition lost those Essential Powers without which a general Government was a mere Sound—The original D(esig)n[114] of Confederation materially different.

p. 29   Dickenson—repeats some Reasons already urged—for Motion.

    Bedford—Objects to these Powers because an undue Weight is intended to be given[115] to some States—Pennsylvania and Virginia are intended to have one third of Representation—The smaller States will be so unconsequential in the general Scale that their Interests will be uniformly sacraficed whenever they are adverse to those of larger States, and the Voice of the solitary Member from Deleware it is not probable will be attended to.

    Adjourned till to Morrow.

SATURDAY, IUNE 9TH

    Met pursuant to Adjournm't.

    Gerry moved to reconsider Appointment of *Executive*—agreed tò reconsider it—He then moved

p. 30 that the Executives of the several States should elect national Executive—and that each Executive should have the same Number of Votes in the Election as the State he represents has Members of the first

---

[113] M. has practically this phrase, but Y. seems to have misunderstood it.

[114] M. and Y. have "draft" in this phrase, but L.'s abbreviation seems to be "Dn".

[115] L. first wrote "it will give an undue Weight"; then crossed out "it will give", and inserted "is intended to be given" after "Weight".

Branch.[116] Reason—Fewer Persons greater Responsibility.[117]

Randolph—Necessary to cloathe national Executive with every possible Confidence—this cannot be obtained in any Mode more effectually than by Election by national Legislature.

Is it probable that all the Executives will[118] be disposed to promote the Growth of the large Oak which is to reduce them to insignificant Shrubs?

p. 31 Individual Executives not qualified—they have not the Information—their Interests are distinct. It is not their Interest to elect the best Men to fill that Station—It must also cause a *periodical Interregnum.*

On Question—10 Noes—Deleware divided.[119]

The 11*th* Resolve was then read—Upon which Mr. Brearly called for the 2*nd* general Proposition marked C.[120]

Brearly—This Mode of Representation just if all considered as one Nation[121]—but if State Distinctions still obtain—if Measures are pursued to perpetuate their seperate Interests—let the whole be di-

116 Y. does not specify which house is to be used as a basis for determining the number of votes, but M. reports the resolution as giving the state executive the same number of votes as his state has in the *Senate*. The Journal omits the clause giving the state executives different numbers of votes.

117 This argument is not given by M. or Y.

118 L. started to write "pro[mote?]" here, and then crossed it out.

119 M. has only 9 Noes, but the Journal and Y. agree with L.

120 No other source mentions the reading of the 11th Resolution. The "Proposition marked C", may be found on p. 113. It calls for representation in the national legislature in proportion to "Quotas of Contribution or to the number of free Inhabitants".

121 This phrase is given by no other authority.

vided into Districts of nearly equal Size and Numbers of Inhabitants—but in our present Situation the Interests of the Smaller States must be sacraficed.

p. 32 He had made a calculation of the relative Representation which had been repeatedly hinted at which need only be read to enable us to determine the probable Consequence—this was on Number of free Inhabitants.[122]

Georgia	1	South Carolina	6
Deleware	1	North Carolina	6
Rhode Island	2	New York	8
New Hampshire .	3	Connecticut	8
New Iersey	5	Maryland	6

Massachusetts	14
Pennsylvania	12
Virginia	16

He was appointed to give foederal Powers—but these too extensive.

Patterson—Powers of Convention inadequate to this System. Confederation is Basis of our proceeding.

Representation exemplified by two Men possessing different Shares of Property—both have a Vote —but the Man of Property has more to protect by

---

[122] This table is not given by M. and Y., although they agree that Brearly thought that Virginia would have 16 votes and Georgia 1. Paterson had a copy of a table something like this in some notes which Farrand thinks belong to this day, June 9. Farrand also notes the existence of such a table among the Wilson papers. The Paterson and Wilson tables include an estimate of the population of each state, and give Maryland 8¾ representatives instead of 6.

p. 33 Government and he has greater Influence.[123] Equal Division of Territory[124]—Hints had been thrown out by Gentleman from Pennsylvania (Wilson) that a new Confederation between some of States would be formed—If Iersey would not be inattentive to her Interest—that State never would agree to the present System.

Wilson—If Confederation dissolved either *Majority* or *Minority* may Confederate.

Compound Ratio of Property and Numbers would perhaps be best to determine Representation[125]—Pennsylvania has not yet been taught to adapt itself to the Scale of Representation proposed by Iersey[126]—

p. 34 sey[126]—Never will—The States are now as in State of Nature[127]—Each Individual ought to have an equal Weight in Government. He has no Authority to divide States.

He will uniformly vote against every State Establishment.

Postponed.

Adjourned till Monday.

[123] That is, if there is no reason why a rich man should have more votes than a poor one, there is no reason why a large state should have more votes than a small one.

[124] According to M., Paterson took up Brearly's challenge to the larger states, and said that if they wanted a *national* system the old boundaries must be changed to make the states equal in population.

[125] M. and Y. report Wilson as saying that representation should be based on numbers, though M. adds that wealth or numbers would give the same result.

[126] Neither M. nor Y. report this irritating phrase, though they agree that Wilson flatly refused to accept equal representation.

[127] According to M., this argument ran that as men who are equal by nature must give up equality when they form civil government, so the sovereign states must give up equality when they form a federal government.

IUNE 11TH—MONDAY

4*th* Resolve *e* considered.[128]

Mr. Sherman—moved that Right of Suffrage be determined by Number of free Inhabitants in each State.—This Motion not seconded.

Each State ought to have one Vote—Individual States to be considered as representing *House of Lords*.[129]

Governor Rutlege moves *that Representation*[130] *be apportioned to Contribution.*

p. 35   King—moves *that Representation*[131] *be not apportioned by the Rule mentioned in the Confederation—but that some other equitable Mode be adopted.*

Franklin—It does not follow that because States in Union are unequally represented that therefore the greater Representation will oppress the lesser. Instances *Great Britain*.[132]

On Question on Mr. King's Motion—Affirmative 7 States. Negative—New York, New Iersey and D(eleware)—Maryland divided.

Mr. Rutlege's Motion then considered[133]—

[128] See p. 113. This seems to be an error, as the debate continued on the question of representation.

[129] According to M. and Y., Sherman's proposal was that in the House each state should be represented in proportion to its free inhabitants, but that in the Senate each state should have one vote.

[130] In the first branch (M. and Y.).

[131] "in the first branch" (Journal and Y.).

[132] That is, the fears of the Scots when the Act of Union was passed, by which Scotland was given only a few representatives in Parliament. This is a very incomplete account of Franklin's rather long speech. Y. gave it little more space, but it may be found in full in M.

[133] The motion was that representation should be according to "the quotas of contribution" (Journal).

Dickenson—Quota of Contribution would throw too great a Share of Power in State that pays most—which Power may be directed to exempt itself p. 36 from Contribution. Taxes, Contributions and Impost collected in the State ought to be Criterion.[134]

Butler—Individual States ought to retain distinguished Marks of Sovereignty—Let them levy Tax.[135]

Wilson—There are some great national Objects to be attained by Government so constituted as this is supposed—Post Office an important one.[136] Moves that Representation of the first Branch be in Proportion to the free Inhabitants and 3/5 of all others.

Gerry—If Negroes represented why not Horses and Cows—Slaves not to be taken in under any Idea of Representation.[137]

Question on Wilson's. 10 States Affirmative, one Negative.[138]

p. 37   Sherman moves that in the second Branch of Legislature each State have *one Vote*.

5 Ayes—6 Noes.

Ayes—New York, New Iersey, Connecticut, Deleware, and Maryland.

[134] This speech is barely indicated by Y. and M. M. puts it earlier, before Franklin's.

[135] Omitted by M., but confirmed, in substance, by Y.

[136] The drift of the argument was, according to Y., that representation in proportion to contributions of the states was impossible, since some national revenue would come from national institutions, such as the Post-Office, and could not be credited to any state.

[137] M. copied this argument from Y. Y.'s accuracy is confirmed by L.'s using almost the same words.

[138] This seems to be a mistake. M., Y., and the Journal agree that the vote was 9 to 2.

That second Branch be apportioned as the first.
On Question 6 *Ayes*—5 *Noes*.

11*th* Resolve that a Republican Government and etc.[139]

Mr. Reed moved that *Government* be obliterated and the *Constitution and Laws of each State* be inserted.

Mr. Madison moved that those Words be inserted after *Government*.

Agreed to Mr. Madison's M(otio)n.
Agreed to strike out Words scored.[140]

p. 38   13*th* Resolve agreed to.[141]

14*th* Resolve—[142]

Randolph—There is no Constitution that does not contravene Confederation[143]—Iudicial Officers sworn to observe Constitution[144]—Wherever Na-

---

[139] This resolution guaranteed a republican government and territorial integrity to each state. See p. 117. L. first wrote "a Republican Constitution and Laws" and then crossed out the last three words and substituted "Government". Probably in his rough notes he had copied the resolution as amended.

[140] See p. 117. The underlined words, which were struck out, were the ones guaranteeing the territory of each state. According to the Journal, the resolution as finally amended read: "Resolved, that a republican constitution and its existing laws ought to be guaranteed to each State by the United States."

[141] This resolution stated that "provision ought to be made for the Amendment of the Articles of the Union . . . and that the assent of the national legislature ought not to be required thereto." All other authorities agree that only the first clause was accepted, the second being postponed.

[142] This resolution required "legislative, executive and judiciary Powers within the several States" to take an oath to support the articles of union.

[143] This statement is not given by M. or Y., though M.'s account suggests it.

[144] That is, *state* judicial officers are already sworn to support *state* constitutions.

tional and State Views are opposed those of State will be prefered.[145]

15*th* Resolve—[146]

Question—5 Ayes, 3 Noes, and two divided.

Connecticut, New York, and New Iersey *No*.[147]

4*th* Resolve was then considered.[148] The Words *for the term of*

Sherman moves that Members of the first Branch be elected every Year.

Rutlege—Triennial Election perhaps best,[149] but moves that the Words *two Years* be inserted in Blank.

Ianifer—moves *three Years*.

p. 39   Madison—Instability of popular Government his Reason for wishing three Years.

Distance of Extremities of Union renders it necessary. The Lessons the Representatives have to learn another Reason.

Gerry—If you fix this at three Years how long must Senate be elected for.[150]

---

[145] After some further debate, the resolution was passed.

[146] All other authorities agree that events described from this point to the top of p. 42 occurred on June 12. The 15th Resolution stated that "the Amendments which shall be offered to the Confederation by the Convention ought at a proper Time or Times after the Approbation of Congress to be submitted to an Assembly or Assemblies of Representatives recommended by the several Legislatures to be expressly chosen by the People to consider and decide thereon."

[147] This agrees with Y. and the Journal. M. has 6 Ayes.

[148] As Y. explains, the Convention now went back to the resolutions which had been postponed, or in which the wording of certain clauses had not been determined.

[149] Neither M. nor Y. gives this opinion of Rutledge's. They simply state that he suggested a two-year term.

[150] Neither M. nor Y. report this sentence. Instead, they record Gerry as making a strong protest against abandoning annual elections.

Madison—Public Opinion fluctuating—it has no Standard—is changing Rapidly.

Local Attachments and temporary Opinions ought to be laid aside.[151]

Question on *three Years*.

Aff. 7 Ayes—4 Noes.

Agreed to strike out Clause limiting Age—10 Ayes—1 No.

Motion to insert *fixed* after *liberal*.

Affirmative 8—Negative 3.

p. 40   Franklin—Moved to strike out *liberal*—carried.

Pierce—moved to add *to be paid out of national Treasury*.

Affirmative 6—Negative 5.[152]

Question on Paragraph to Word Service.[153]

8 Ayes—3 Noes.

Gerry moved after *Service and* to insert *under the national Government*.[154]

Carried unanimously.

In Blank after *Space of* agreed to insert *one Year*.[155]

C. Pinkney Moved to strike out *to be incapable*

[151] This speech was in answer to a remark by Gerry that public opinion would not tolerate triennial elections. The last sentence is not paralleled in M. or Y.

[152] All other sources agree that the vote on this motion was 8 to 3.

[153] The remaining part of the paragraph, next debated, provided that Congressmen should be ineligible to any state or federal office during the term for which they were elected, and for some period thereafter.

[154] This motion is reported by no other authority. However, M. states that an amendment was made.

[155] That is, Congressmen are to be ineligible for state or federal office until one year after the expiration of their term. L. omits a motion to delete this whole clause.

and etc. to the End of Paragraph.[156] Struck out unanimously.

Age of Members of second Branch fixed at *thirty*.

p. 41   *7 Years* moved by Governor Randolph[157] Duration of Office of second Branch.

Mr. Pierce against—it will give too much Alarm.

Sherman for *5 Years*.

Question on *7 Years*.

8 Ayes—1 No and 2 divided.

N.B. New York divided, Iudge Yates being in *Negative* and *I* affirmative.[158]

Rutlege moved seconded by Butler[159] that the Clause resp(ectin)g Pay of second Branch be struck out.

3 Ayes—7 Noes—1 divided.

Connecticut, Deleware, and South Carolina Aye, Massachusetts divided.

Question on whole Clause, 10 Ayes—1 No.[160]

9th Resolve resp(ectin)g Iudiciary considered.[161]

---

[156] The clause struck out would have made immediate reelection of Congressmen impossible, and would have subjected them to recall. Y. does not specify which of the Pinckneys made the motion, and M. merely inserted Y.'s statement "that Mr. Pinckney moved".

[157] M. says Spaight made this motion.

[158] Apparently L. was suffering from accusations that he always followed Y.'s lead, and wanted to record his independence.

[159] The Journal agrees with this; M. and Y. give Butler as proposer of the change.

[160] This clause applied to the Senators the rules concerning ineligibility to other offices, already drawn up for Representatives. M.'s account for the rest of this day's proceedings is taken from the Journal, and Y.'s account is incomplete.

[161] See p. 116.

Piracies and Felonies on the High Seas *struck out*—so *Captures from Enemy.*

p. 42   C. C. Pinkney moved to insert after *Foreigners* to insert *or Citizens of two distinct States of the Union.*[162]

Postponed.[163]

Adjourned till to Morrow.

IUNE 13TH

Met according to Adjournm't.

9th Resolve—

Mr. Randolph moved that the *9th* Article shall extend to Collection of national Revenue Impeachment of any national Officers and Questions which involve the national Peace and Harmony.[164]

Agreed to.

7th Resolve[165]—Mr. C. Pinkney moved that the Words to be chosen by the national Legislature be inserted in the Blank left for that Purpose.[166]

p. 43   Madison moves second Branch to appoint.

Question carried.[167]

6th Resolve that each Branch ought to possess Right of originating Acts.

[162] This motion passed (Journal).

[163] The part of the resolution postponed was that which established supreme and inferior federal courts.

[164] This motion displaced all the earlier attempts to define the jurisdiction of national courts. Y. gives it, but M. copied it from the Journal.

[165] This is an error; the question was on the appointment of judges, that is, on the 9th resolution.

[166] No other authority specifies that this was *C.* Pinckney. The Journal records the motion as one for appointment by the upper house alone, but M. and Y. agree with L. and their statement is probably correct.

[167] That is, judges to be appointed by the Senate.

Mr. Gerry moves Exception as to the upper House *excepting* Bills to supply to public Treasury.[168]

8 Noes—3 Ayes.[169]

Committee reported.[170]

Copies of Report ordered—Consideration postponed.

Adjourned till to Morrow.

IUNE 14TH

Met—on Motion of Mr. Patterson adjourned.[171]

IUNE 15TH

Met according to Adjournm't.

p. 44   Mr. Patterson moved Resolves—which I seconded.

Mr. Madison supposed it would be proper to commit them to a Committee of the whole House. After some desultory Debate agreed to.

Butler—Moved to go into Committee immediately.[172]

I moved for the Morning. I declared that tho I had hitherto given my Vote without joining in the Debates my Sentiments were unaltered—our sole Object ought to be foederal—that these Resolutions

---

[168] That is, the Senate is not to originate money bills. There was an extensive debate on this motion, which may be found in Madison.

[169] This agrees with the Journal. Madison recorded only 7 Noes.

[170] This refers to the report of the Committee of the Whole on the Virginia Resolutions. Lansing copied the report into the back of his note-book, see pp. 109 *ff*.

[171] Paterson requested this adjournment in order that he and his associates might have time to prepare a different plan of union.

[172] This motion is not mentioned by other authorities.

afforded an Opportunity of fairly contrasting the
p. 45 Systems, but as the one had been an Object which
had engaged the Attention of the Committee a considerable Time—the other recently introduced the
House was not prepared to give it that Investigation
which its Importance merited.[173]

Randolph spoke in Favor of it. Madison, Wilson, Williamson and Butler against it.[174]

Question unanimously carried.—Copies ordered.
Adjourned till to Morrow.

Saturday, June 16

Met according to Adjournment.

I stated the difference between National and
foederal Systems—the first subjects all to the Con-
p. 46 troul of the general Government and draws its Representation from Individuals—the foederal has its
Representation from States collectively and subjects
great foederal Concerns to general Government.

The one involves a total Subversion of State
Sovereignties—the other delegates only Part.—I
urged that the Confederation ought to be the Basis
of our System. This Power now contended for too
great to be given by Implication.[175] Improbable that
so many individual States should adopt same Language to describe an Intention which cannot be inferred from the wording of it.

[173] M. gives no details of this speech. Y. gives an outline
which agrees fairly well with L.'s version.

[174] No other authority mentions this debate.

[175] That is, power to propose an entirely new constitution.
As L. goes on to say, the credentials of most of the state
delegations gave power only to propose amendments to the old
articles.

It may be objected *Union* one of the Articles subject to Revision. But the distinct Sovergnties essential to constitute it.

p. 47   [176] Two Reasons assigned—one that public Mind ripe for System. 2ndly that it must accomodate.

If public Mind to be collected from public Acts instead of being fluctuating—it has been uniform a considerable Time.

Impost an Instance—Most States annexed Clauses expressive of their Distrusts.[177] What Reason to suppose Change?

If public Mind to accomodate it must either happen gradually—then useless—suddenly—then Effect of some great Commotion—it cannot be controul'd or directed.

p. 48   The national System proposes two Houses.

All Reasoning on Systems unaided by Experience has generally been productive of false Inferences.

Why go into unexplored Ground?

The new Government will be regarded with that Iealousy inseperable from new Establishments. Congress is a body respected and known.[178]

---

[176] Six words were carefully crossed out here. They seem to be "and draws its representation from individuals". These words occur at the top of p. 46 of L.'s note-book. He may have been interrupted while copying his notes, and have started to repeat himself when he began work again.

[177] According to Y. this referred to the attempt made by Congress in 1783 to get permission from the states to tax some imports for 25 years and to raise $1,500,000 annually from the states. Few states granted unconditional assent, and New York refused to act. M. copied his account of this sentence from Y.

[178] Y. has "the prevalent opinion of America is, that granting additional powers to Congress would answer their views." In general M. and Y. agree with L.'s version of his own speech, but some details are found only in his report.

Patterson—has proposed his Plan.

1. Because it accords with Powers.

2. With Sentiments of the People.

If we wish to meet Approbation walk in Sphere assigned to you.

Practicable Virtue preferable to finest theoretic System.

Larger States have agreed that each should have one Vote. They cannot recal their Assent.

(In two last Sheets—)[179]

p. 68   IUNE 15TH[180]

Patterson—Maryland and Iersey came last into Confederation.[181]

Wilson's Principles applied to States totally wrong.[182]

If you will form national Government equalize

[179] Lansing had copied into the back of his note-book the Virginia Plan and the report of the Committee of the Whole (see pp. 109 ff.). At this point he reached these insertions, so the rest of the debate had to be put in the last two pages of the note-book.

[180] This should have been June 16. Lansing wrote June 15th on p. 45 (at the beginning of this debate), and then corrected it, but he forgot to make the change here.

[181] The argument was that the large states came into the Confederation quickly, in spite of the equality of suffrage, of which they were now complaining, and that the small states, who theoretically benefited by the agreement, came in reluctantly (see M.).

[182] Y. "The doctrine advanced by a learned gentleman from Pennsylvania, that all power is derived from the people, and that in proportion to their members they ought to participate equally in the benefits and rights of government is right in principle but . . . wrong in application to the question now in debate.

"When independent societies confederate for mutual defence, they do so in their collective capacity; and then each state for those purposes must be considered as one of the contracting parties."

the States and throw all your public Lands in common.

Two branches of Legislature unnecessary—Congress is competent—the additional Powers ought therefore to be exerted by them.

The Expence of national System another Objection.[183]

p. 69 Wilson—compares Plans.[184] Observe their relative Merits must be drawn from Experience and Reasoning.

Powers he will first consider.

Supposes himself authorized to propose every Thing—but can conclude Nothing.

State Sovergnties not Idols of People.

A Citizen of national Government will not be degraded.

From every State we hear Complaints that their Governments are inadequate.

Does not mean to collect Sentiments from conversing with People—let the System go to the States —and let them consider it.[185]

Would give *Congress* Power with great Reluctance—

1. Congress is not on Principles of a free Government derived from People.

p. 70 2. Because only one Body.

[183] According to Y. and M., Paterson was especially worried by the expense of the large number of representatives who would be necessary. M. and Y. have much fuller reports of this speech. Paterson took some phrases of this speech from his notes for a speech on June 9, see Farrand I, 185 *ff.*

[184] M. and Y. give the details of this comparison.

[185] M. reports Wilson as saying that one of the great merits of the Virginia Plan was the provision for ratification by the *people.*

Inequality in Representation is a Poison which will contaminate every Branch of Government.

Great Britain Iudicial not appointed by a venal Parl't—the Iudicial uncorrupt—Not so House of Commons.[186]

United States another Instance—Rhode Island one.[187]

Executive ought to be single.

Triumvirate cemented by Interest—Kings of Sparta and Consuls shew necessity of single Executive.

C. Pinkney—Discovers if Iersey had a single Vote would agree to national System.

Our Powers only recommendatory.[188]

Grecian Confederation—*Lycia League*—23 Towns—Some had 1 others 2 and the largest 3 Votes.[189]

p. 71   Governor Randolph—The Resolutions from Virginia were drawn under Conviction of reforming Confederation.

If Powers not competent ought not to hesitate.

This a great Occasion—Step boldly beyond prudential Rules.

---

[186] And the House of Commons is corrupt because representation in it is unequal (M. and Y.).

[187] Wilson had given the example of a small Dutch province blocking the wishes of the majority (M. and Y.). According to M., he hinted that the United States had such members; according to Y., he openly named Rhode Island. Naturally Y. and L. would take pleasure in recording an insult to one of the small states, while M. might be anxious to forget it.

[188] Therefore anything can be proposed.

[189] This remark is not reported by other authorities. Pinckney later suggested that representation in the Senate should follow this example.

King of France unpaid, Creditors ruined, and Soldiers languishing.[190]

We would be Traitors to our Country if we did not embrace this parting Angel.

States not Objects of Coercion.[191]

If done by distressing Trade—*some not commercial*—by Inroad—tardy, expensive and dangerous.

Members of Congress particularly dependent on their own States.

This last attempt to confederate—[192]

Adjourned.

[190] Not given by M., but in Y. and other reports (see Farrand, I, 263 *ff*.).

[191] That is, as he goes on to say, it would be difficult to coerce the States, which was part of the New Jersey Plan (M.).

[192] Rather, this is the last opportunity to confederate (M. and Y.).

p. 1   NAMES OF MEMBERS OF CONVENTION

> *[1]Nathaniel Gorham
> *Rufus King   Massachusetts
> *Elbridge Gerry
> *Caleb Strong
>
> *Wm. S. Johnson
> *   Elseworth   Connecticut
> *Roger Sherman
>
> *Robert Yates
> *Alexander Hamilton   New York
> *Iohn Lansing Iun.
>
> *Gov. W. Livingston
>   Abraham Clarke
> *William Houston[2]   New Iersey
> *Wm. Patterson
> *Thomas Brearly C. I. (Chief Justice)
>
> *Iames Wilson
> *President B. Franklin
> *Thomas Mifflin
> *Robert Morris   Pennsylvania

[1] The asterisk seems to mean that the member had attended the convention while L. or Y. were present; that is, before July 10. No New Hampshire delegates are listed because none came before L. left.

[2] L. has confused William Houston of Georgia and William C. Houston of New Jersey.

p. 2

*George Clymer
*Iared Ingersoll
*Governeur Morris   Pennsylvania
*Thomas FitzSimmons

*Iacob Broom
*George Read
*Gunning Bedford   Deleware
*Iohn Dickenson
*Richard Bassite

*Iames McHenry
 Iohn F. Mercer
 Daniel Carrol   Maryland
*Daniel of St. Thomas
   Ianifer
*Luther Martin

*George Mason
*General George Washington
*Gov. Edmund Randolph
*Iames Madison   Virginia
*George Wythe
*Iames Blair
*Iames McClurg

*Gov. Alexander Martin
*Richard Dobbs Spaight   North Carolina
*Hugh Williamson
*Wm. Richardson Davie

p. 3

*Gov. John Rutlege
*Charles C. Pinkney   South Carolina

*Pierce Butler
*Charles Pinkney

*Wm. Churchill Houston[2]
 Gov. George Walton
*William Few   Georgia
*William Pierce
*   Baldwin

p. 4 Iournal continued

Iune 18th

Met according to Adjournment

Dickenson—wishes the terms *national* and *foederal* to be exploded—Moves to strike out *foederal Constitution* out of Iersey Propositions and alter it so as to read *so as to render the Government of the United States adequate to the Exigencies Preservation and Prosperity of the Union.*

Agreed.[3]

Hamilton—The Situation of the State he represents and the Diffidence he has of his own Iudgment induced him to Silence tho his Ideas are dissimilar from both Plans.

p. 5 No Amendment of Confederation can answer the Exigencies of the States. State Sovereignties ought not to exist—Supposes we have Powers sufficient—Foederal an Association of States differ-

---

[3] The Journal, which is the only other source for this action of Dickinson's (since M. merely copied the Journal), says that Dickinson moved to postpone consideration of Paterson's first resolution, and offered the substitute given above for discussion. The Convention agreed to postpone, not to accept Dickinson's resolution. Reports of the next day's proceedings show that the Journal is right.

ently modified—[4] Diet of Germany has Power to legislate for Individuals—In United States Confederacy legislate for States and in some Instances on Individuals—*Instances Piracies*. The Term *sole* he supposes was to impress an Idea only that we were not to govern ourselves, but to revise Government.[5]

Another Difficulty that the Legislature cannot be supposed to have delegated a Power they did not possess themselves—So far as Respects the State of New York one of the Branches of the Legislature considered it—It was *said they might have Recourse to the People*—this had its Influence and it was carried by one Vote.[6] We ought not to sacrafice the public Good to narrow Scruples. All America, all Europe, the World would condemn us. The only En-

p. 6

[4] "Different Confederacies have different powers and exercise them in different ways." (M.)

[5] Farrand, III, 579. The credentials of the New York delegation read "that three delegates be appointed . . . for the sole and express purpose of revising the Articles of Confederation . . ." *Ibid.* 14. The resolution of Congress authorizing the Convention contained the same expression.

Y. gives a somewhat different version of this remark: "the manifest import is no more than that the institution of a good government must be the *sole* and *express* object of your deliberations."

[6] This argument is not clearly reported in any of the authorities, but Hamilton's line of reasoning seems to have been as follows:

The State Legislatures may not be able to ratify the new plan of government because of constitutional limitations and the general principle that no government can diminish its own sovereignty. In that case the revised articles may be submitted to the people. Some legislatures had this in mind; for example, in the New York Senate it was moved that no act of the Convention should be binding if it was repugnant to or inconsistent with the Constitution of the State. The motion was *lost* by only one vote, because it was felt that the people could ratify any change even if the state legislature could not.

quiry ought to be what can we do to save our Country.—Five Essentials indispensible in foederal Government.—1. A constant and active

Interest.

2. Utility and Necessity.
3. A habitual Sense of Obligation.
4. Force.
5. Influence.[7]

Every Set of men who associate acquire an *Esprit de Corps*. This will apply forcibly to States—they will have distinct Views—their own Obligations thwart general Good.

Do not we find a Iealousy subsisting? In the State of New York we had an Instance—The last

p. 7 Requisition was partially paid—the principal Part of their Funds applied to discharge State Obligations[8] —the Individual States hostile to general Interest.

Virginia will in 25 Years contain a Million of Inhabitants—It may then be disposed to give up an Union only burthensome.[9] The Distribution of Iustice presents itself to every Eye—this has a powerful Influence and must particular attach Individuals to the State Governments.[10]

Two Modes of Coercion—of Laws—of Military.

Individuals are easily controuled—not so Society—You must carry the Force to Individuals—

---

[7] These main heads are found in all authorities, except that M. has "love of power" for no. 2. This is clearly wrong, as Hamilton's own notes show.

[8] This specific attack on New York was omitted in M., and not fully reported in Y.

[9] This refers to point 2 above.

[10] This, according to M., refers to point 3.

If only State[11] delinquent it would cause a war— If more they would associate and make a common Cause of it.[12]

p. 8   We must resort to Influence—Dispensations of Honors and Emoluments of Office necessary—these are all in the Hands of the State Governments—If they exist in State Governments their Influence too great.—our Situation is peculiar—*It leaves us Room to dream* as we think proper.[13]—Groecian Confederacy lost for Want of adequate Powers—German the same. Swiss Cantons—general Diet has lost its Powers.[14] Cannot combine States but by absorbing the *Ambition and Avarice* of all.

Iersey Propositions—Regulating Trade[15]—Revenue not adequate to meet our Debt[16]—where are we to find it? Requisitions—the several States will de-
p. 9   liberate on them.—Requisitions founded on Quotas must always fail. There is no general Standard for Wealth in Communities—Pennsylvania and North Carolina[17]—Connecticut and New York compared.[18]

[11] L. probably meant to write "if only *one* State".

[12] While this version agrees in general with other reports, L. is the only one who makes clear the distinction which Hamilton was trying to make between the ease of controlling individuals and the difficulty of restraining organized societies.

[13] This sentence seems out of place here. It may have come earlier in the speech. It is not reported or suggested by other authorities.

[14] L. has greatly abridged Hamilton's historical arguments. They may be found in fuller form in M.

[15] That is, about all that the New Jersey Plan grants is power to regulate trade.

[16] That is, the revenue produced by the New Jersey Plan will be inadequate.

[17] Quotas based on land are unjust; compare Pennsylvania with North Carolina (M.)

[18] Quotas based on number of inhabitants will be equally

New York derives great Wealth from Commerce—Connecticut none—Indirect Taxation must be multiplied.

Equality of Suffrage ruinous to the Union.

Doubts ˙have been entertained whether the United States have a Right to build a Ship or raise a Reg(imen)t in Time of Peace—this Doubt might involve almost our Ruin.[19]

The Organization of Congress exceptionable—They are annually appointed and subject to recal.—They will of Consequence represent the Prejudices p. 10 of the States not general Interests—No Power will be executed if the States think proper to obstruct it. If general Government preserves itself it must extinguish State Governments.

If Congress remains Legislature the Sovereignty must ultimately vest in them.[20]

The Expence of national Government is a Consideration with him—it will probably amount to £100,000 per ann.—this however surmountable—It will not do to propose formal Extinction of State Governments[21]—It would shock public Opinion too much.—Some subordinate Iurisdictions—something

unjust; compare the relative wealth of citizens of New York and Connecticut.

[19] And the New Jersey Plan provides no remedy for this (M.)

[20] M. reports this argument as follows: "The general power whatever be its form if it preserves itself, must swallow up the State powers, otherwise it will be swallowed up by them. . . . Giving powers to Congress must eventuate in a bad Government or in no Government."

[21] The line of thought here, according to M. and Y., was that the expense of maintaining the national government might be compensated for by the gradual extinction of state governments.

p. 11 like limitted Corporations.[22] If general Government properly modified it may extinguish State Governments gradually—Representation is another difficulty.[23] British Government the best—Dispairs of ever uniting (?) the great Objects of Government which have been so successfully attained by the British, public Strength and individual Safety, in any Republican System. He thinks here it would support itself[24]—the Citizens of America may be distinguished into the wealthy well born and well educated —*and the many*. If Government in the hands of the latter they sacrafice the few[25]—are as often in the wrong as right.

You can only protect the few by giving them exclusive Rights—they have Nothing to hope from p. 12 Change—Monarchy is essential to them.[26] One Branch of Legislature ought to be independent to check popular Frenzy—or Democraties will prevail. —Seven Years is no Check[27]—It is no Object for

[22] That is, while district courts and local corporations will always be necessary, most of the machinery of state government could be eliminated without doing any harm (M.)

[23] That is, the problem of getting able men to accept the duties of a representative (M. and Y.)

[24] "If it was once formed it would maintain itself" (Y. and King). M. omits this phrase. On the other hand, Y. and L. omit Hamilton's remark (reported by M., King, and in Hamilton's notes) that it would be unwise to propose anything but a republican government.

[25] Hamilton also said that if government was in the hands of the few, they would oppress the many (M. and Hamilton's notes.)

[26] According to Hamilton's notes, his argument was that if there were separate representation of the few and the many they would need "a mutual check. This check is a monarch." Therefore create an executive as much like a monarch as possible.

[27] That is, a seven-year term for senators.

Men of first Importance—Little Daemagogues will fill Assembly—Undertakers your Senate.

In Republics trifling Characters obtrude—they are easily corrupted—the most Important Individuals ought to drawn forth for Government—this can only be effected by establishing upper House for good Behaviour. Congress are Objects of foreign Corruption.[28]

Executive ought to be during good Behaviour— p. 13 He will part with his Power with Reluctance. You ought to interest him in the Government.

This may be objected to as establishing an elective Monarchy—but he will be liable to Impeachment for mal-conduct. The Election it supposed would cause Tumults—To avoid this the People in each District should chuse Electors—those should elect a few in that (?) State who should meet with Electors from the other States and elect *the Governor*.

Roman Emperor—elective—by Army

German Emperor—by great Electors.

Polish King—great Barons who have numerous Dependents.[29]

These were tumultous from their Institutions— We may guard against it.

p. 14   The principal Citizens of every State are tired

[28] Both M. and Y. report Hamilton as saying that the "weak side of a republican government is the danger of foreign influence" and a corresponding phrase is found in his notes. The flat charge of attempts to bribe Congress is found only in L. It was perhaps suggested by Hamilton's tone, but it seems doubtful that he actually said it.

[29] According to M., the argument was that elective monarchies had always been bad because the wrong people had the power of electing.

of Democracy—he then read his Plan and expatiated on it—See[30]

Adjourned till to Morrow.

IUNE 19TH

Met according to Adjournment.

Madison—The Distinction between foederal and national Representation—the one from the State collectively—the other from the People is not well taken—There are two States in the Union in which Delegates are chosen by the People.

Probability of adopting Plan—We must adopt such an one as will ensure Safety—Let us have a

p. 15 Chance.[31] Confederation on same ground as Compact made by a Number of Persons—If one violates it all are discharged—in Treaties it is agreed that a Breach of any[32] is a Dissolution of all—Iersey has refused to comply with Requisitions—He is anxious to perpetuate Union—but will not consent to prolong it on its present Principles.—How is Confederation observed?

Georgia has entered into War and made Treaties in express Violation of Union.[33]

Virginia and Maryland entered into Compact in like Violation.—Massachusetts has a regular Body of Forces without Approbation of Congress.

[30] L. intended to make a reference to his copy of Hamilton's plan, inserted in the last pages of this volume.

[31] The first 3 sentences of this paragraph are not in M., but are reported by Y.

[32] "the breach of any one article" (M.)

[33] Transactions with the Indians were reserved to Congress, yet Georgia made war on them. In M.'s version of the speech, he crossed out a specific reference to Georgia, but Y. and King agree that Georgia was named in the speech.

The conciliatory Resolution of Congress resp(ectin)g Wioming Dicision evinces Weakness of general Government.[34]

p. 16 The Power retained by the different States Executives of pardoning would alone defeat national Government. The Amphictionic Council had a Right of judging between Members, mulcting Aggressors—drawing out Force of States—and several other important Powers—The Confederacy was however of very short Duration.[35] It will not be denied that the Convention has as much Power as Congress—They have exercised it in recommending a new Rule of Apportionment—11 States agreed to it.[36]

Martin—before the Confederation each State had complete Sovereignty—When confederated they met so and they must remain equal.[37]

p. 17 Wilson—The Declaration of Independence declares the U.S. collectively to be vested with Power of making War and Peace—this antecedent to framing Constitutions consequently paramount.[38]

[34] Connecticut's claim to the Wyoming Valley in central Pennsylvania was denied, but Congress awarded compensation to Connecticut to persuade her to accept the decision.

[35] M.'s own version of the speech does not contain these details, but Y. and King both report them.

[36] The reference is probably to the attempt made by Congress in 1783 to get each state to agree to make an annual contribution, based on population.

The argument contained in these last three sentences is found in no other authority. This is peculiar, since on the whole L.'s version of this important speech is very incomplete and omits many important arguments.

[37] L.'s notes for the rest of this day are confused and report events out of their proper order. This speech and the following speeches by Wilson and Hamilton were made after the votes recorded later on.

[38] M. reported this argument in a weakened form: "observing that the United Colonies were declared to be free and inde-

Hamilton—agrees with Wilson—this is calculated to destroy many Heresies in Politics—How is general Government to affect Interests of smaller States?—In Agriculture, Commerce and Revenue— large States are remote from each other—Commercial Interests are not the same—on what Principle can they combine to affect agriculteral Interest?[39]

Motion by Wilson to move that the Committee rise and report that it is the Opinion of the Committee that the Plan submitted by New Iersey is inexpedient[40]—This was accordingly done and I was disposed to submit to it because the Sentiments of the Committee on the Question of Representation in the first Instance could not be pointedly taken.[41]

On the first Resolve when Question put—6

p. 18

pendent States; and inferring that they were independent, not *Individually* but *Unitedly*. . . ." Y. comes closer to L., but is not so definite. A very full report of Wilson's speech by King (Farrand, I, 331) shows that L. understood the point better than M. or Y.

[39] M. reports Hamilton as saying that no combination of large states was to be feared, but omits the proof given here. Y. apparently misunderstood the argument; he has: "The three great objects of government, *agriculture, commerce* and revenue, can only be secured by a general government."

[40] This step was taken before the three speeches, reported above, were made. The motion is ascribed to King by Y. (and by M., copying Y.). From this point on, debate was in Convention and not in Committee of the Whole.

[41] L., and several of his associates, felt that the real issue was whether the States were to have equal, or proportional representation in Congress, and that the New Jersey Plan confused this issue because it included other principles which could easily be attacked. Therefore, the small states gave no very ardent support to Paterson's proposals, only three (New York, New Jersey, and Delaware) voting for it. L.'s explicit statement of the shift in strategy is interesting. From this point on, the minority, as he suggests, tried to center the debate on the question of representation.

States Affirmative—4 against and Maryland divided.[42]

The first Resolution was then considered—(Mr. Elseworth moved)[43] after some Debate on it.

Adjourned till to Morrow.

IUNE 20TH

Met according to Adjournment.

Elseworth moved that first Resolve be amended so as to read that the Government of the United States ought to consist of a Supreme Legislative Iudiciary and Executive.[44]

p. 19 Agreed to.

The second Resolve was then considered.

Lansing—moved that it be postponed to take up the following—*"Resolved that the Powers of Legislation be vested in the United States in Congress."* Sherman seconded Motion.

Explained Reasons why the Question on the Propositions from Iersey was not urged—It was brought forward to shew the general Principles on which we would determine. It was however found it could not discover Sentiments of Committee—this will bring it to a Point.[45]

[42] This must refer to the vote on Dickinson's substitute for Paterson's first resolution, which was *lost* by a vote of 6 to 4, with Maryland divided.

[43] The words in parentheses were crossed out. As may be seen by looking below, they belong to the next day's debate. L. apparently copied his notes for several days into the journal at one time, and was sometimes confused as to where the break between the proceedings of two days came. See above, p. 14.

[44] This eliminated the irritating word "national" from the first resolution as reported by the Committee of the Whole. See p. 109.

[45] This paragraph was not reported by any other authority. See above, p. 70, and note 41.

I have urged two Reasons—1. Incompetency of p. 20 Powers. 2. Public Mind not prep(ared?) The first —general Assertions have only been made that we have Powers—but most Gentlemen seem to have given it up—one Gentleman has offered the Mode of App(ointmen)t in two States as an Argument[46]— Whatever Mode is adopted they are still Representatives of Sovereignties. Another Gentleman[47] admits Incompetency of Powers but will step forward with a generous Confidence. To imitate him we must be convinced of Utility of System—We must be certain that it will secure important and equal Benefits to all.

If destitute of these Convictions we should be Traitors to our Country.[48]

It is said to be unimportant because merely recommendatory.[49]

p. 21   Let us examine some of Objections to vesting Powers in Congress.

1. Inequality of Representation—Britain has been instanced to prove Evils. So has R. Island. Neither of these applicable.

The Boroughs contain few Inhabitants much impoverished—or the Property of some Man of large Estate. These easily corrupted but it is not from

[46] M. had said that the representatives of two states in Congress were chosen by the people. See above, p. 68.

[47] Randolph, see p. 57.

[48] This statement is reported by no other authority.

[49] Wilson had argued that, since the Convention could only recommend, limitations on its power were unimportant. According to M., L. replied to this argument by saying that any recommendation "of so respectable a body must have a great effect, and if it does not succeed, will be a source of great dissentions." L. forgot to record at this point his argument (in M.) that the public mind was unprepared for a strong national government, as shown by the opposition of the States to federal taxes.

hence to be inferred that several Thousands can be corrupted with equal facility.

Counties in England unequal in *Extent Population* and Wealth. No Complaints from that Source. Rhode Island acted without Confederation—She had a Right to deliberate and to dissent.[50]

p. 22   But Congress represent *State Interests and Prejudices*. However Representation modified that will be the Case. One Branch appointed in same Mode —the second is intended to be composed of Men avowedly of a less liberal Turn—[51]

It has been said there can be no Inducements for large States to oppress small—If there are no seperate Interests why so solicitous ab(ou)t Represent(atio)n. The Share of Virginia to Deleware as *16* to *1* in Arithmetic Proportion—but in political as *40 to 1* at least.[52] This Legislature to legislate in every Case—they cannot have the necessary Information.[53]

p. 23   But Congress is more easily corrupted? To obviate this only one Observ(ation). One appointed annually subject to recall—the other for 7 and 3 Years absolute.[54]

[50] Rhode Island refused to grant the federal government permission to levy a tax on imports. M., as usual, left out this specific reference to a State.

[51] A line has been erased here, the last word of which was "System". The meaning of this last sentence is not quite clear. Unfortunately neither M. nor Y. record anything which sounds like it.

[52] This last phrase was not reported by any other authority. M. omitted the whole sentence.

[53] According to M. and Y., L. was thinking of the power to veto any state law conferred on Congress in the Virginia Plan.

[54] That is, in the old Congress, members held office for only one year, and could be recalled at any time; in the new, they

As long as State Sovergnties exist each much[55] an equal Suffrage—this is equitable—it is necessary.[56]

On the new System cannot reason from Experience

Coercion—in both Systems equal as to their Objects.[57]

Mason—Want of Power strong Objection if we could conclude. We ought to risk it—In Eventual Treaty with G. Britain our Commiss(ioners) did so —Met Approbation of their Country.

No Gentleman can think Citizens of America will trust their Powers to one Set of Men—Will they trust to a *Conclave*, subject to Corruption—certainly not.[58]

p. 24   In 1778, 79, and 80 Factions in Congress.— States have refused to give Congress Power because one Body, and not elected by the People.

There will be no Coercion in this Government.[59]

He will not consent to Abolition of State Sovereignties.

Martin—The Legislatures have refused to give Congress Powers—no Objection could exist with them that People did not appoint.

would have longer and more secure tenure, and would feel safer to take bribes. This argument was reported by no other authority.

[55] Probably a slip of the pen for "must have".

[56] This sentence was not reported by M. and Y.

[57] M. and Y. have nothing which would explain this statement.

[58] This argument had a double force. It was meant to answer L.'s argument that the refusal of the States to give Congress power to tax showed the unwillingness of the people to accept a strong federal government. It was also meant to show that expedients such as the New Jersey Plan were bound to fail (M. and King).

[59] The New Jersey Plan contained a provision authorizing the use of force against recalcitrant States.

10 States must be injured by App(ortionmen)t of Representation. Coercion as compleat in one System as the other. If U.S. only exercise Powers which are not Objects of Odium and leave the Residuum to the individual States they must become completely odious and the Consequence is evident.[60]

p. 25 Sherman—one Body is sufficient—the great States supposed themselves benefited by Confederacy —Virginia adopted it without a dissenting Vote— Massachusetts had no Objection. Would be content to have two Houses if one represented States.

W-n-[61] We go contrary to the Principles of App(ortionmen)t if we submit to limit it to one Branch.   On Question

	6 Negative	*Affirmative* 4
	Massachusetts	
	Pennsylvania	Connecticut
	Virginia	New York
Maryland divided	North Carolina	New Iersey
	South Carolina	Deleware
	Georgia	

Upon the President's rising to put the Question on original Resolution Bedford moved an Adjournment.

p. 26 Question 5 for—6 against it[62]—The State of Deleware then put off Question—Adjourned till to Morrow.

[60] This rather brief report of Martin's speech stresses remarks which were passed over by M. and Y., for example, the idea that the residual powers left to the States (such as justice) would make them odious. It omits many of the legal arguments used to justify state sovereignty.

[61] Wilson. This brief note hardly gives a fair idea of Wilson's speech.

[62] The Journal, the only other source which mentions this vote, gives 4 Ayes and 7 Noes.

Iohnson—Individuality of States ought to be preserved—You deposit Aristocratic and democratic Power in different Bodies[63]—And we can deposit more but then let one Branch represent Sovereignties.

Wilson—As States represented Individually[64]—their Sovereignty to be preserved—Quantum of Power preserved in smaller States as comprehensive as in larger[65]—It will be the Interest of all to represent general Government *if Interest of any*—of Consequence they will co-operate.

p. 27   Madison—Legislature of States have not shewn Disposition to deprive Corporations of Priviledges—Why should they here.—Question carried d(ivide)d as Yesterday.[66]

C. C. Pinkney moves that 3rd Resolve[67] be so altered as to read ought to be appointed *in such Manner as the several Legislatures shall direct*—he supposes this will give greater Satisfaction to the People.

Hamilton—If you permit Legislatures to elect you will have *State Interests* represented.

Govr. Rutlege—Legislatures of States ought to appoint—The Representation will be more refined—Whether the People elect themselves or appoint others to elect substantially the same.

Wilson—Official State Influence will defeat

---

[63] This remark is reported by no other authority.

[64] That is, members of the second branch are to be chosen by state legislatures, so each state has individual representation.

[65] This argument is not reported by other authorities.

[66] L. first wrote "Question for it passed", and then erased these words. The question was on the second resolution, that the Legislature consist of two branches.

[67] On the election of members of the lower house.

p. 28 the Object of national Government if Election by Legislatures.

King—same Sentiment differently expressed.

Question — Negative — Massachusetts, N e w York, Pennsylvania, North Carolina, Georgia

Affirmative—Connecticut, New Iersey, Deleware, South Carolina.

Maryland divided.[68]

N.B. Iudge Yates and Colo(nel) Hamilton in Negative—I was for Affirmative.[69]

Randolph[70] moved to obliterate *three Years*[71] and insert *two*.

Sherman[72]—for *one Year*[73]—By suffering them to remain three Years they accomodate their Sentiments to those with whom they associate—they must be oblidged to return Home every Year to remind them of what they owe their Constituents.

Mason—By having annual Elections remote
p. 29 States would generally be unrepresented in Beginning of Sessions.

Hamilton—The Opinion of the People is fluctuating—You must exercise your Iudgment, convinced that the Pressure of unavoidable Circumstances will direct the public Mind.

[68] L. forgot to record Virginia as voting No.

[69] L. is again interested in showing his independence. See pp. 50, 83. This vote of the New York delegation is interesting for another reason, since Mason later remarked (Farrand, III, 367) that neither Y. nor L. ever voted with Hamilton, and this annoyed Hamilton so that he went home.

[70] L. forgot to record that before this motion the Convention agreed that the first branch should be elected by the people.

[71] As the term of office for members of the first branch.

[72] Several speeches recorded by M. are omitted here.

[73] M. has "Mr. Sherman preferred annual elections, but would be content with biennial." Y. agrees with L. in stating an unqualified preference for one year terms.

Listlessness prevails in New York on Acc(oun)t of annual Election[74]—Consequence is that Factions are represented in that Government.

Adjourned till to Morrow.[75]

Iune 22

Did not attend Convention being indisposed.

p. 30

Iune 23rd

3rd Resolve—*to be paid out of the public Treasury*

Question—five Ayes—five Noes—1 divided.

"to be ineligible to any Office established *by a particular State or* under the Authority of the United States."

C. C. Pinkney moves to strike out *by a particular State or.*

Wilson—If you strike out these Words you confirm Attachments to particular States and give that Attachment a Direction injurious to a general Government.[76]

Sherman—If State and general Governments have seperate Interests their Iealousies will be mutual and they already operate very powerfully—hence you must leave the Individual States much Power.

p. 31 Gorham—It is necessary to give general Government Energy—prevailing Opinions are too democratic.[77]

---

[74] M. omits the specific reference to conditions in New York. Y. agrees with L. in giving it.

[75] Before adjournment a two-year term was substituted for the proposed three years.

[76] Not reported by M., but given by Y.

[77] This speech reported by no other authority.

Question—Ay 8—No 3.

Madison moves after *established* insert *or Emoluments whereof shall have been augmented by the Legislature of the United States during the Time they have been Members or within one Year thereafter*[78]—He wishes Executive to have App(ointmen)t of Officers—He thinks it necessary to hold out Inducements to Men of first Fortune to become Members.[79]

Butler—Executive may be as corrupt as Legislature—It would place too pervading an Influence in him.[80]

Rutlege—We ought not to wish to have place Hunters in Legislature—No Incentives ought to be held out to Men of that Description—Honesty will probably predominate in lower House Ability in the upper.[81]

p. 32   Mason—He has experienced in Virginia that whenever a Man of the first Character who was not a Member of the Legislature was opposed to a despicable one who was a Member—the latter uniformly succeeded. If the Restriction is continud a Seat in the Legislature will lead the Way to first Offices—this sufficient Inducement—he is against Amendment.

Madison—Men of Ability are not found (?)

[78] This motion referred to ineligibility of members of the lower house to office under the federal government. L.'s wording differs from M.'s, but is supported by Y. and the Journal.

[79] According to M.'s motion, members could be appointed to any office existing before their election.

[80] Not in M., but a similar statement was reported by Y.

[81] No other authority reports this last sentence.

in Virginia to step forward in Public. Persons of other Descriptions press for Admission.[82]

King—Venality may be as successfully applied in the Appointment of Relations of Members as Members themselves.

p. 33   Wilson—*Selfish Characters* will endeavor to place *Men of a generous Turn of thinking and Men of Abilities* in a Situation not to be appointed[83]— Executive ought to have app(ointmen)t.

Question 2 Ayes 8 Noes—Maryland divided, *Iersey and Connecticut ay.*

Sherman moves after ineligible to insert *and incapable of holding.* Unanimously agreed.

The Question was then put[84] on the Words *for the Space of one Year after its Expiration.*

4 Ayes—6 Noes—1 divided.

Adjourned till Monday.

p. 34   IUNE 25TH

4th Resolve.[85] C. Pinkney—We are peculiarly situated—We have no Distinction of Ranks—When Executive hereditary or elective for Life Peers necessary. Not above *100* Men in the United States so rich as to be dangerous—these cannot be considered as a distinct Class on a national Scale—three Classes

[82] Therefore eligibility to federal office should be allowed as an inducement. M. puts his speech somewhat later in the debate, but Y. agrees with L. in placing it here. Y. and L. are probably right, since the speech (even as reported by M.) is a direct answer to Mason's remarks about the Virginia Legislature.

[83] This argument is omitted by M., but given by Y.

[84] Before this question, the Convention had already voted that members of the lower house should be ineligible for federal office during the term for which they were elected.

[85] This resolution dealt with the composition of the upper house.

—professional Commercial and agriculteral—there Interests now generally resolvable into the last. He is therefore for something like the Virginia System, but State Sovereignties must be retained.[86]

p. 35 The United States too extensive to furnish a general Legislature competent to the Management of domestic Concerns. States ought to be divided into five Classes—to have *from one to five Votes*.[87]

Reed—The Confederacy similar to Articles of Co-partnership—Articles insufficient—before they are revised adjust old Accounts—apply all Lands *acquired and protected by common Arms to discharge public Debt*—this done we may make another Agreement.

Wilson—The System of Hen. IV to unite Europe as a Republic had trifling Objects to those we are now engaged in attaining—The Happiness of *the Globe* involved in it—he has distinct Ideas of State and general Government—has Objection to any Part of Legislature being elected by the State p. 36 Legislatures—it will *perpetuate local Prejudices*— States are not intended as component Parts of general Government—they need not be represented— The Objects of national Government will be—Commerce—War—Treaties Coins and other great national Concerns. On those Occasions the Proportions of Representation so as to give each State a proper Weight in the Government may be preserved, in the second Branch as well as the first.

[86] A very full report of the speech to this point (furnished by Pinckney) may be found in M.

[87] This last paragraph is not in M. Y. agrees with L.'s report in general, but does not give the specific proposal recorded in the last sentence. Pinckney repeated this proposal on July 2, see p. 101, and note 165.

If both Branches are elected from same Source they will have same Interests.—Moves that the second Branch be elected *by Electors to be elected by the Citizens of the United States.*

p. 37   Elseworth—Every Representative will have local Ideas however elected. No existing and distinct Interests to form Ballances—Republican Governments cannot exist throughout U.S. but by support of individual States. Virginia cannot give Law to Kentuckey. Massachusetts cannot extend her Government 100 Miles from Capital. These are strong Instances against an Extension of Republican Government on a general Scale—but the Inhabitants of every State are warmly attached to their several Constitutions[88]—this another Reason.

Iohnson—Individuality of States ought to be preserved.[89]

p. 38   Mason—If Self Defence necessary to general Government it will be as necessary to individual States.—this can only be done by representing the States.

On Question on Wilson's Motion—lost.

Question *on Election by Legislature.*

9 Ayes—2 Noes.

Agreed to expunge *sufficient to ensure their Independence.*[90]

7 Ayes—4 Noes.

Duration of Senate then considered—*seven Years.*

[88] This phrase omitted by M., but given by Y.
[89] This phrase is in Y. and was copied by M. from Y.
[90] Copied by M. from Journal, but not given by Y.

Gorham—wished the upper House to be formed into Classes.[91]

p. 39   Randolph assents—State Governments will be perpetually tending to the Subversion of general Government.—this would give general Government Consistency.

Reed—good Behaviour would be more effectual —If Mr. Hamilton would make the Motion he will second him.

C. C. Pinkney—thinks 4 Years sufficient—otherwise Representatives might be induced to become Inhabitants of State in which Seat of Government established.

Madison—this will weaken it too much.[92]

On Question on striking out *seven Years.*

7 Ayes—3 Noes.

Gorham moved 6 Years—5 Ayes—5 Noes—1 divided. (H[amilton] and myself voted Neg. on Question.)[93]

p. 40   On Question *five Years.* 5 Ayes—5 Noes—1 divided.

Morris moved that the Senate should be elected for and continue in Office during good Behaviour. Not seconded.[94]

Adjourned till to Morrow.

[91] So that a certain number would retire every year. Y., and M. copying Y., say this was agreed to at this point, but Journal says that no vote was taken.

[92] Omitted by M., but given by Y.

[93] This was written in the margin, and from its position might refer either to this vote or the one just preceding. However, since both M. and the Journal agree that New York voted Aye on the first question and No on the second, it must refer to the latter. This is another case in which L. voted against Y., and in which Hamilton was supported by one of his colleagues.

[94] This is probably an error. According to M., Morris seconded Read's motion for life tenure given above.

IUNE 26TH

Reed moved to insert *nine Years* in the Blank.[95]

Madison—The Advantages of Government cannot be extended equally to all—Those remote from Seat of Government cannot be placed in a Situation equally advantageous with such as near it[96]—Distinctions will always exist—that of Debtor and Creditor—Property had made Distinctions in Europe before a Nobility was created—Inequality of Property p. 41 will produce the same Distinctions here—The Man in affluent Circumstances has different Feelings from the man who daily toils for a Subsistence. The landed Interest has now the Supreme Power—a Century hence the commercial may prevail[97]—The Government ought to be so organized as to give a Ballance to it and protect one Order of Men from the predominating Influence of the other.—The Senate ought to represent the opulent Minority—If this is not done the System cannot be durable.

Sherman—Permanency and Security appear the great Objects of pursuit—In Connecticut have had annual Elections for 135 Years[98]—It has protected Property effectually and no Imputations of Instability on it.

p. 42   Hamilton—We are now considering the Cause of Democracy[99]—he is attached to a free Government and would chearfully *become a Martyr to it*— The occasional Violence of Democracy and the uni-

---

[95] M. and Y. put a motion for six years first, but the Journal confirms L.

[96] These first two sentences have no parallel in M. and Y.

[97] Omitted in M.; given in Y.

[98] M. "more than 130 years"; Y. "132 years".

[99] Both M. and Y. have "republican government."

form Tyranny of a Despot are productive of the same Consequences.—to prevent them he is for tuning the Government high—In the ordinary Progress of Things we must look to a Period as not very remote when Distinctions arising from Property will be greater—You must devise a Repository of the Rights of the wealthy—At Rome after the Institution of the tribunitian Power greater Distinctions arose from the unequal Distribution of Riches and *Rich* and *Poor* were more oppressive Distinctions

p. 43   than *patrician* and *plebeian*. Under the Colonial Government of Connecticut its Objects were contracted —but we have taken a new Station—Its Powers ought to be enlarged in Proportion to the Magnitude of the Objects it is intended to embrace. He will therefore go beyond any of the Ideas advocated by either Party.—Is for nine Years.[100]

Wilson—Foreigners in making Treaties will naturally be inclined to wish a permanent Body to treat with—This will give their Measures Respect and Permanency—Great Britain will not make Treaty with us because Congress instable.—*2nd* Branch have that (?) Power.

On Question Delaware Georgia[101] and Pennsylvania Aye—8 Noes.

Gorham moves *six Years one third to go out biennially.*

7 Ayes—4 Noes—New York New Iersey South Carolina and Georgia No.

p. 44   C. C. Pinkney—moves that *to receive fixed*

[100] These last two sentences are not in M. or Y.
[101] The Journal and M. have Virginia as the third state voting Aye, and record Georgia in the negative.

Stipends be struck out[102]—It is the prevailing Idea that *2nd* Branch ought to represent the Wealth of the Nation—If so they ought to serve without Compensation.

Franklin—Is of the same Opinion—We will always be able to command the Attendance of a sufficient Number of Men, whose Wealth will enable them to serve Gratis[103]—On Question 5 Ayes—6 Noes.

Elseworth moves *To be paid out of the State*[104] *Treasurys.*

Madison—by making Elections six Years distant from each other we evince a Disposition to make them independent.—this can only be done by a Payment from national Treasury.

p. 45   Strong—If you fix the Provision it will not comport with oeconimical Ideas of the Day—It will alarm the Public—Let Legislature provide for themselves.[105]

On Question 5 Ayes—6 Noes.

to be paid out of the Treasury of the United States.

Mason—The second Branch is intended as a Check to the democratic Spirit—Would it not be best to insert *a Qualification of Estate?*

On Question[106] 5 Ayes—6 Noes.

to be ineligible *to any Office by any particular State.*

---

[102] M. copied this motion from Y. or the Journal.

[103] This sentence is omitted in M. and Y.

[104] L. wrote "general" first, then crossed it out and substituted "State".

[105] This speech was not reported by M. or Y.

[106] As to paying Senators from the treasury of the United States.

On Question 3 Ayes—8 Noes.

or United States during the Time for which they were elected and for one Year thereafter.

p. 46   On Question—Unanimously affirmative.[107]

5*th* Resolve[108]—carried unanimously without Debate.[109]

Adjourned till to Morrow.

IUNE 27TH

Rutlege moves that 6*th* Resolve be postponed to take up 7*th* and 8*th*.[110]—Agreed to.

7*th* Article—the Words *ought not to be according to the Rule established by the Confederation* first to be considered.

Martin—general Government only intended to protect State Governments.

National Objects for Legislative and Executive Exertion ought to be defined and much contracted.

p. 47 If after the greatest Caution defective, it may be revised by a future Convention.

While national Government acts for general Good in the Sphere prescribed for it—no hostility to be apprehended from individual States—it will receive their Patronage and Protection.

The Respect shewn *to a general Government* weak to Excess evinces the amicable Disposition of the Individual States to it.

Virginia and Maryland made Convention for

---

[107] L. first wrote "6 Ayes" and then erased it.

[108] That each branch have the right of originating acts.

[109] This vote was omitted in M.'s original draft, but he inserted it from the Journal or Y.

[110] These resolutions established representation according to population in both branches.

settling Navigation in *Chesepeak and Potowmack*—this is no Breach of Confederation.

The Troops of Massachusetts were drawn out to quell Rebellion—Neither of those Instances prove a p. 48 Disrespect to Articles of Union.[111]

In every Confederation Equality of Suffrage indispensible.

The larger States have more to protect and their superior Wealth and Strength give them a proportionate Influence.

The three larger States can carry the most injurious Points to the other States—unless the others miraculously combine.

The Executive and Iudicial will be from them. The Executive has a Right to subject Laws to a Revision—this will protect them effectually.[112] But p. 49 what is to prevent them from making decided Arrangements to assume all the Power of general Government?[113]

Athens—Sparta and Thebes pursued same Line of Conduct.[114] From the Iournals of Congress it appears that Virginia was sole for apportioning Representation by Numbers or Contribution—She has gained many Proselytes since.

The smaller States gave up their Share to the common Territory acquired by their joint Exertions—this was an important Sacrafice.[115]

[111] M. had claimed on June 19 that these actions were a breach of the Articles of Confederation, see above, p. 68.

[112] That is, the ten smaller states could never pass, over a veto, a law injuring the three larger states.

[113] Most of the speech from this point on was omitted by M., but the same ideas are found in Y.'s report.

[114] That is, of depriving small states of equality in voting.

[115] An answer to the Virginia contention that the large states

Iersey Maryland and several other States have contributed as essentially to repel the Enemy as the large States who now suppose themselves entitled to Preeminence—he would not trust a Legislature so constituted to legislate for Carolinian Slaves or Massachusetts Oxen.—the one was to form Part of Rule for Representation—He cannot give his Assent to subject the Rights of Freemen to them.

p. 50

It has been observed that great States have great Objects, which they will not permit the small States to thwart—If those Objects are directed to general Good they will be pursued by all—if not, it would be right to defeat them.[116]

Adjourned till to Morrow.

IUNE 28TH

p. 51

Martin—It is in State Capacities we are taxed—The Majority of States ought to tax.

In arguing it has been said that Protection ought to be extended to *rich* and *poor*—they ought only to protect States. Daily Experience shews the Genius of People is in Favor of small Governments—they are for seperating whenever they are remote from its Seat.

In Amphictionic Council each State had two Votes. Sparta attempted to exclude three Cities.

Destruction of Confederacy owing to large States.

In the Dutch and Swiss Confederacies each has one. Berne and Zurich are equal to all the Rest—each has one Vote.

alone made a sacrifice in accepting the Articles of Confederation with their provision for equality of votes.

[116] This last paragraph was not reported by M. or Y.

Happiness is preferable to the Splendors of a national Government.[117]

p. 52

Admission of large States into the Confederation dangerous to the others if they are admitted on Principles of perfect Equality—but more so if they have a constitutional Predominance.

There is no Danger of not having another Convention unless the Conduct of the present prevents it.[118]

The greater States as now circumstanced are not Objects of Terror.

Massachusetts convulsed—Pennsylvania Commerce in the Power of Iersey and Deleware—Virginia weak and divided.[119] It is as much their Interest to confederate as any of the smaller States—If they will not do it on the Footing of Equality let them take their own Course.

p. 53

Madison—Fallacy of Argument owing to a Connection of Legislative Ideas with Right of making Treaties.[120]

Are the larger States congenial to each other by Proximity common Interests or Similarity of Pursuits?—They are not—they are so situated as to perpetuate Diversity of Interests.

The Staple of Massachusetts is *Fish* and she has

[117] This sentence not reported by M. or Y.

[118] This sentence not reported by M. or Y.

[119] These specific references to the weakness of the larger states were not recorded by M. or Y., although each hints at them.

[120] That is, while large and small European states could make a treaty for the regulation of commerce on an equal footing, the case would not be the same if they formed "a Council . . . with authority and discretion to raise money, levy troops, determine the value of coin and etc." M.

carrying Trade—that of Pennsylvania *Wheat* and Virginia Tobacco.

Equality will uniformly excite Iealousy—Did Rome and Carthage combine to destroy their Neighbours?

This Question will determine whether we shall confederate at all or partial Confederations shall be formed.[121]

Williamson—Mathematically Demonstrable that Representation ought to be proportioned to Individuals.[122]

If the Taxes are laid by smaller States what would prevent them from surcharging the greater?

p. 54   Wilson—Is it not unjust that old Sarum should send two Members and London only four? If this admitted it applies forcibly to the present Case.

Lansing—moved that Word *not* be struck out.[123]

Madison—Efficient Government can only be formed by apportioning Representation.

The States may be equalized by general Government.[124]

---

[121] This is a very brief account of M.'s rather long speech. See M. and Y.'s reports.

[122] This agrees with Y. M.'s version is that it was mathematically demonstrable "that if the states were equally sovereign now, and parted with equal proportions of sovereignty, that they would remain equally sovereign."

[123] Both M. and Y. record this motion as made immediately on the conclusion of Martin's speech. The motion would have made the 7th resolution read "the right of suffrage in the first branch *ought* to be according to the rule established by the Confederation."

[124] M. gives no indication that he made a second speech this day. Y. and Paterson, however, report him as speaking twice. The opinions given in this second speech are recorded by M. as the last paragraph of his first speech.

The State of New Iersey being unrepresented by
the Indisposition of Governor Livingston the Question was put off by New York.[125]

Previous to which L. . . . . (erased).

Adjourned till to Morrow.

p. 55   IUNE 29TH

Iohnson—Must unite Ideas of *States* with Districts of Country containing a certain Number of
Inhabitants.[126]

Gorham—three Members of Massachusetts are
Descendants of Persons who resided in three different Provinces now united in Massachusetts—this Cir-
cumstance does not influence their Measures. If all
the States go off excepting one—Massachusetts will
stay with that one and recommend System.[127]

Reed—Has no Doubt resp(ectin)g it—will
agree to Report so far as respects this Point.[128]

Hamilton—In the Course of his Experience he
has found it difficult to convince Persons who have

[125] Not given by Y., but copied by M. from the Journal.

[126] M. ". . . as in some respects the States are to be considered in their political capacity, and in others as districts of
individual citizens, the two ideas, instead of being opposed to
each other, ought to be combined . . ." Y. misreports this
speech. He has "States are political societies. For whom are we
to form a government? for the people of America, or for those
societies? Undoubtedly for the latter." King confirms L. and M.

[127] This is a somewhat abbreviated report of a very blunt
speech, in which Gorham remarked that Delaware and New
Jersey could not preserve their independence if the Confederation
were dissolved.

[128] This is not quite accurate. M. and Y. agree that Read
said that he favored proportional representation only if the new
government were "truly national," but that he feared the mix-
ture of state and federal powers. He favored Hamilton's plan.

been in certain Habits of thinking.[129] Some desultory Remarks may not be improper. We can modify Representation as we think proper.

The Question simply is, what is general Interest.

p. 56 Larger States may submit to an Inequality of Representation to their Prejudice for a short Time—but it cannot be durable.[130] This is a Contest for Power[131]—the People of all the States have an Inequality of Representation.[132]

So long as State Governments prevail State Influence will be perpetuated.

There may be a Distinction of Interests but it arises merely from the carrying and noncarrying States.

Those Persons who have had frequent Opportunities of conversing with the Representatives of European Sovereignties know they are very anxious to perpetuate our Democracies. This is easily accounted for—Our weakness will make us more man-

p. 57 ageable. Unless your Government is respectable abroad your Tranquility cannot be preserved.

This is a critical Moment of American Liberty —We are still too weak to exist without Union. It is a Miracle that we have met—they seldom occur.

[129] This somewhat irritating introductory sentence is not in M., but is suggested by Y.

[130] M. omitted this sentence, but it is given, in milder form, by Y.

[131] M. ". . . it is a contest for power, not for liberty. . . . The State of Delaware . . . will lose power . . . but will the people of Del. *be less free.* . . ."

[132] M. and Y. put this sentence earlier in the speech. The argument was that since each state modified representation by property qualifications, etc., representation in the country as a whole might be arranged as the Convention saw fit.

We must devise a System on the Spot—It ought to be strong and nervous, *hoping* that the good Sense and principally *the Necessity of our Affairs* will reconcile the People to it.[133]

Pierce—The Difficulty of carrying on Business in Congress is owing to local Prejudices and Interests. Must sacrafice States Distinctions.[134]

Madison—Examine Iournals of Congress—see whether States have been influenced by Magnitude. p. 58 Small States have embarrassed us—Embargo agreed to by twelve States during the War—Deleware declined it.[135]

On Question whether *not* should be struck out. Massachusetts Pennsylvania Virginia North Carolina South Carolina and Georgia—Noes.

New York—New Iersey. Connecticut and Deleware—Ayes. Maryland divided.

Question put on Resolve[136] carried—6 Ayes—4 Noes—1 divided.

Elseworth—moves to postpone Remainder of *7th* Resolve to take up the *8th*.[137] Question 9 Ayes—2 Noes.

---

[133] This last paragraph is not in M., but is paralleled in Y.

[134] Copied by M. from Y. Y. gives a fuller version of this speech.

[135] This speech is out of place here. It was made after the vote recorded below, and formed part of M.'s speech at the end of the day's proceedings. The mistake was probably caused by the fact that M. spoke twice on this day. L. had no record of his first speech, but remembering that he spoke twice, he divided the second speech in two.

[136] "That the rule of suffrage in the 1st branch ought not to be according to that established by the Articles of Confederation." The vote was only on this clause, not on the whole resolution, which laid down a new rule for representation.

[137] That is, before discussing the new rule for representation in the first branch, he wanted to secure an equal vote for each state in the second branch.

Elseworth—In first Branch you draw Representation from Numbers—the Individuals will have their Rights protected here.

He will move that *each State have an equal Vote in second Branch.*

This will preserve State Sovereignties—

p. 59   In any Community select a fifth, a tenth, or any other Proportion from all the different Classes of Citizens—give them an exclusive Right of governing—they will become a distinct Order and oppress the Rest. So it will be with the States.

It will be much easier for the three States[138] to confederate than the others to join to defend themselves.

Baldwin—wishes Powers to be modified[139]—but Property ought to be represented in one Branch—

Madison—If there was any Difference of Interests would agree to equal Representation.

Let Gentleman recollect the Experiments that have been made to amend Confederation[140]—they always miscarried. The Dutch Republics made four

p. 60 several Experiments all ineffectual.[141]

Adjourned till to Morrow.

[138] That is, the three large states.

[139] According to M. and Y., Baldwin was against Ellsworth's plan, but thought that the powers of the national legislature should be defined, and limited, before the question of representation was discussed.

[140] According to M., Ellsworth had suggested making a compromise now, and perfecting the Constitution later. Y. understood M. as referring to unsuccessful attempts to amend the Virginia Constitution; King thought that M. was talking about attempts to reform the Amphictionic League.

[141] The fragment given above (see note 135) should be added to the end of this speech. M. has no record of this second speech, but it is given by Y. and King.

IUNE 30TH

Mr. Hamilton left Town this Morning.

Brearly—moves that President write to Executive of New Hampshire to send Delegation.[142]

Question. New York and New Iersey Ayes— 5 Noes 1 divided.

Each State shall have equal Vote.—Wilson— Gentlemen[143] have declared the Reluctance of Eastern States to acceed to national Government.—If a Minority are inclined to seperate it never can be on stronger or better Principles.[144] State of Votes now as *22* to *90*[145]—Shall the one fourth controul the Remainder.

Can we forget for whom we form Governments —for Men not imaginary Beings called States.[146]

p. 61   Elseworth—On this Occasion each State has only a preventative Vote—the Minority is not to govern but to prevent its own Destruction—this is not novel—it is useful.

It is said the Equality of Suffrage has embarrassed us—Can Gentleman Instance salutary Measure being lost by not having a Majority of States in its Favor.

[142] According to M., this was an effort to secure the vote of another small state. The opposition felt sure that New Hampshire would be for equal representation in the upper house.

[143] Ellsworth, on June 29.

[144] That is, the *majority* can never have better ground than this.

[145] M. "The votes of yesterday against the just principle of representation were as *22* to 90 of the people of America."

[146] This is a rather brief account of a very vigorous speech. The last sentence was suggested by a remark of Hamilton's on June 29: "But as States are a collection of individual men which ought we to respect most, the rights of the people composing them, or of the artificial beings resulting from the composition."

Rhode Island did not defeat Impost under Confederation.[147] If Security be the principal Object of the great States they have it here.

All the Reason[148] in favor of national Government founded on Ideas of State Interests having too powerful Operation—as they are permitted to exist they must still influence.[149]

p. 62   Madison—Equality of Representation was dictated by the Necessity of the Times.[150] The larger States cannot be safe unless they have a greater Share in Government. Connecticut has shewn a Disregard to her foederal Compact[151]—She has declined complying with Requisition.[152]

Elseworth—That Connecticut has not complied with Requisition is owing to her superior Exertions during the War—to keep her Regiments compleat she incurred an enormous Expence—She was exhausted—that was Reason of Delinquency.[153]

Sherman—That Legislature of Connecticut did not comply with Requisition is no Impeachment of

[147] The argument, according to King and Y. was that the impost did not fail because it lacked a majority in Congress, but because it involved amendment of the Articles of Confederation.

[148] "of" was crossed out here.

[149] And therefore the small states will still need protection against the selfish interests of the larger ones.

[150] This sentence is not in M. or Y., but is confirmed by King.

[151] According to M., Ellsworth had appealed to "the obligations of the federal pact which was still in force . . . persuading himself that some regard would still be paid to the plighted faith under which each state . . . held an equal right of suffrage. . . ."

[152] This is a very inadequate account of M.'s long speech. See M. and Y.

[153] This paragraph was not in M.'s original notes, but he later copied similar remarks from Y.

p. 63 Congress. If the Argument is to have any Weight shew that the State frustrated it in Congress.[154]

Davie—90 Members are proposed for Senate— As States accede the Numbers will be much encreased—this will embarrass—they ought to be less.

The Preservation of the State Governments is the only Object of Confederation.[155] but if each State has a single Vote it will defeat the whole System.[156]

Wilson—he subscribes to Iustice of Davies Remark—the Senate ought to consist of a few. In apportioning Representation he will agree that every p. 64 100,000 Persons shall be represented by one Member and that every State having less should have one.

Franklin—We must do like a Ioiner in making a Table—take off the Protuberances—pare the different Opinions to a common Standard. He has prepared a Proposition with that Intention—Each State ought to have a certain Number of Votes in Senate.

On some Occasions an Equality of Suffrage to be admitted in States, in others to be apportioned.[157] but thinks Equality is inequitable.[158]

[154] This argument omitted by Y., but given by M.

[155] This sentence not in M., but confirmed by Y.

[156] According to M., Davie liked none of the plans for the upper house. He was against proportional representation because it would make the Senate too large, yet he admitted that an equal vote for each state would bring back all the evils of the old Congress.

[157] Farrand I, 507. In the Franklin papers the suggestion is as follows:

"That the Legislatures of the several States shall choose and send an equal number of Delegates . . . who are to compose the 2d. branch . . .

"That in all cases or questions wherein the Sovereignty of

In the last War the U. States and King of France had not an equal Vote in the Disposition of the Money expended for common Defence![159]

King—Every Vice of the present System will be perpetuated by adopting Amendment—We subject our Minds to imaginary Evils—Is much affected—has heard no Arguments in Favor of it.[160]

Dayton—If Gentlemen will substitute Declamation for Argument it is not surprising that they are unattended to—A Number of Reasons forcible in their Nature have been assigned in Favor of Amendment—they have not been answered. He is convinced this can never receive Approbation of the People.[161]

p. 66   Bedford—Will rather agree to consolidate Government than apportion Representation unequally.

Ambition and Avarice influences us—We represent the different Interests of our States—the larger States wish to aggrandize themselves at the Expence of the others. The Language of the greater States is *give us Power we will exert it for your Benefit.*

If a Combination does not destroy us a Rivalship of the large States will.

individual States may be affected . . . each State shall have equal suffrage.

"That in the appointment of all Civil Officers . . . each State shall have equal suffrage.

"That in fixing the salaries of such officers . . . and generally in all appropriations and dispositions of money . . . and in all laws for supplying the Treasury, the Delegates of the several States shall have suffrage in proportion to the Sums which their respective States do actually contribute to the treasury."

This account of Franklin's suggestion is confirmed by M.

[158] There is no other authority for this statement.

[159] This last paragraph was not in M.'s original notes, but he later copied a similar account from Y.

[160] There is no other authority for this last statement.

[161] The last sentence is not in Y., but is confirmed by M.

p. 65 (appears at left margin beside "France" line)

The smaller States are entrapped—you get a Representation under one *View* you give into another.[162]

Is a Breach of the Union so trifling as to be told with *a Smile*—that a few States will confederate—they dare not—It is only calculated to intimidate.

p. 67   The People expect an Amendment of the Confederation—they will be surprised at our System—they are not ripe for it.[163]

King—When Scotland and England united the same Arguments were adduced—Their Rights however still exist. If there is a Power which from its Prevalence may absorb all others, it will have that Effect whether you confederate or not.

Adjourned till Monday next.

JULY 2ND

On Question for Equality of Suffrage—Massachusetts Pennsylvania Virginia North Carolina—South Carolina for Affirmative and Connecticut New York New Iersey Deleware and Maryland Negative.[164] Georgia divided.

p. 68   C. Pinkney—He is one of those who believes that if Proportion is adjusted in both Branches as in first it will operate in the Mode stated by Minority.

---

[162] That is, the small states sent delegates to the Convention merely to amend the Articles of Confederation so that the federal government could raise money, and they are urged to accept an entirely new system of government.

[163] L. omitted some of the more irritating remarks made by Bedford in a very violent speech, especially Bedford's remark that if the Confederation were dissolved, the smaller states would seek foreign aid and alliances (M. and Y.) See below, notes 168, 176, 177.

[164] As is evident, L. accidentally reversed the vote. The first states voted No, the others Aye.

North Carolina South Carolina and Georgia have Interests different from great States—their Staples are Indigo and Rice.—Must make a Compromise so as to preserve all.

Proposes 4 Classes—States to have from one to four Votes.[165]

G. Morris—*2nd* Branch is Check on the first— to correct Precipitancy, Changeableness and Excess —all these have marked Acts of Congress—*2nd* Branch must be Men of great Property—composed of those Men who are disposed to lord it over the Rest.—We ought to contrive that Men of established Property should fill it—they must be chosen for Life—Aristocracy should keep down Democracy. —It is objected they will immediately do wrong—he believes so—he hopes so—that will form Ballance.[166]

p. 69

[165] This is the only absolutely contemporary description of what Pinckney proposed. M. does not give Pinckney's motion, but merely refers to a document, supposedly describing the plan, which Pinckney sent him many years later. It has since been demonstrated that this document is not contemporary with the Convention. (See Farrand III, 595 *ff*.)

The proposal to divide the states into groups occurs frequently in Pinckney's writings, but usually he seems to think of the groups as mere geographical units. Here he seems to propose that the largest states shall have four votes, the next largest three, and so on. There is a hint of this in M. "How then shall the larger states be prevented from administering the Genl. Govt. as they please, without being themselves unduly subjected to the will of the smaller. By allowing them some, but not a full proportion." See Pinckney's remarks on June 25, above, p. 81, where he proposed that the states "be divided into five Classes— to have from one to five Votes," and the Journal for June 8, where Pinckney moved "that the states be divided into three classes—the first class to have three members, the second two, and the third one member each . . ."

[166] cf. Rutledge's speech on June 23, "Honesty will probably predominate in lower House Ability in upper."

—they ought not to be paid they will pay themselves. The Executive should fill second Branch.

If our Establishments are good they must be supported and will take a proper Direction—If the State Governments have Distribution of Loaves and Fishes the general Government cannot prevail—You must give them Disposition of Offices and *Baubles*—The Senatorship will operate as a Lure.[167]

Governor Randolph—Warmth has formed a Barrier to Conviction[168]—A Security may be offered **p. 70** to smaller States—Executive may correct it by giving him additional Powers—Give second Branch an Equality of Vote in his Election—in Distribution of Offices and in determining on Impeachments[169]—the Executive will be oblidged to interpose in Favor of 2d Branch.

If however every Attempt to make a general Confederation is inefficient it would influence him to seek elsewhere.[170]

Some desultory Conversation then took Place the Result of which was the Appointment of a Committee of a Member from each State to try to settle **p. 71** Representation—the Committee balloted for consisted of Gerry, Elseworth, Yates, Patterson, Frank-

[167] This is a rather brief account of a lengthy speech, but it includes Morris' main points. Everything in it—even the hope that the upper house would do wrong—is confirmed by M. or Y.

[168] According to M., Randolph spoke of the "warm and rash language of Mr. Bedford." Y. has "warmth exhibited in debate."

[169] M. and Y. mention only an equal vote in electing the executive. However, the other two clauses, and especially the last, would be a logical deduction from the first.

[170] M. and Y. do not give this. M. has "he was determined to pursue such a scheme of Government as would secure us agst. such a calamity." Y. approximates this.

lin, Martin, Bedford, Mason, Davie, Rutlege and
Baldwin. Adjourned till Thursday 5*th* Iuly.

IULY 5TH

Mr. Gerry reports from Committee that each
State shall have a Vote in 2*d* Branch, provided it is
generally agreed that every 40,000 shall send one
Member in the first. Money Bills to originate ex-
clusively in lower House.[171]

Sherman—as we are pretty equally divided, it is
best to put Question on the whole.[172]

Wilson—We are not to be misled by Sounds—
there is no equal Division—More than 2/3*ds* of one
Sentiment.[173]

Madison—Altho' the House was equally divided
on the 2*nd* Branch—on the first there was a con-
p. 72 siderable Majority for departing from Equality—
All the Concessions are on one Side—We are reduced to the Alternative of displeasing *Minority* or
Majority—by deciding for the latter we have Nothing to fear—the former every Thing.—He would
rather have a System received by three or four
States than none.[174]

G. Morris[175]—If the smaller States persist, if

---

[171] This line seems to have been inserted after the rest of
the page was written.

[172] The only remark resembling this that can be found in M.
and Y. is ascribed to Martin.

[173] Y. agrees that Wilson spoke at this point, but does not
report these remarks. M. copied Y.

[174] M.'s own version of this statement is: "But if the principal States comprehending a majority of the people of the U.S.
should concur in a just and judicious plan, he had the firmest
hopes that all the other States would by degrees accede to it."
Y. has nothing on this part of the speech.

[175] Yates' notes cease at this point, and a statement was made
in the first printed edition of his notes that he and L. left the

Argument is unavailing, the Sword will determine it.—To overturn the States is impracticable—but you may extract the Teeth of the *Serpents*.—We have been too warm.[176]

Bedford—He has been warm—that not owing to a Want of Respect[177]—but while he acknowledges that he was apparently warm, he cannot help remark- p. 73 ing that he has Reason to be so—The Language of Intemperance is by no Means peculiar to himself.— Gentlemen have threatened in Terms very indelicate, tho' they have generally moderated their Voices when they did so. one Gentleman has declared the smaller States must agree[178] another that *two-thirds* ought to give the Law[179] and a third[180] has pointedly de-clared that Force must be used—Do those Gentlemen suppose that Sentiments of that Kind can produce any other Effect than a Smile—they are mistaken if they do; we know their Language is calculated to make Impressions in favor of their System—but it cannot have that Effect—We know the States who p. 74 have Recourse to it are impotent.[181]

Patterson—same Sentiments differently ex-pressed.

Convention at this time. However, as can be seen from L. and the Journal, Y. and L. continued to attend the Convention through July 10.

[176] This last remark was directed at Bedford. Several other speakers had already expressed their resentment of his last speech. (See note 163.)

[177] Just as L. omitted Bedford's remarks about the smaller states allying themselves with foreign powers, so he omitted here a rather weak attempt which Bedford made to explain away his remark.

[178] Madison (see p. 103). This reference is not in M.

[179] Wilson (see p. 103). This reference is not in M.

[180] Morris, in the speech just made.

[181] These last two sentences are not given by M.

Rutlege moves that Representation in the first Branch be in proportion to Contribution.

Butler seconds it—You may either take this Rule or whole *Number of Whites and Slaves.*[182]

Adjourned till to Morrow.

IULY 6TH

After a Repetition of Sentiments frequently urged before by several Gentlemen it was agreed on Motion of Mr. G. Morris to refer the first Proposip. 75 tion in Report of Committee to a Committee of five[183] —The Motion was carried 9 States against 2. Committee appointed consisting of Mr. Gorham, Mr. Randolph, G. Morris, Rutlege and King.

Adjourned till to Morrow.

N.B. Before the Appointment of the Committee Question was put on Part of Report which had in Object confering the exclusive Right of originating Money Bills in first Branch.

On which Question there were *five Ayes,* three Noes—and 3 States divided—New York Massachusetts and Georgia divided. A Dispute arose whether it was carried in Affirmative—Some Debate on Subject—postponed.

---

[182] Butler's remarks are not given by M. The motion was voted down. L. omitted several speeches at the end of this day's proceedings, and was even more careless on the next three days. Apparently he was getting tired of keeping notes; perhaps because he and Y. had already decided to leave.

[183] L. originally wrote "the Remainder of first Proposition" and then crossed out "Remainder of." The first proposition gave each state one representative for each 40,000 inhabitants. Several members felt that it was unwise to fix a permanent ratio in the Constitution.

p. 76
IULY 7TH

Question whether the last Question was carried in Affirmative. 9 Ayes—2 Noes.[184]

Equality of Suffrage.—After some Debate in which Nothing new was offered the Question was put and carried—6 Ayes—3 Noes—2 divided.

Ayes—Connecticut—New York—New Iersey —Deleware—Maryland and North Carolina.

Noes—Pennsylvania—Virginia a n d South Carolina—

Divided—Massachusetts and Georgia.

Adjourned till Monday next.

IULY 9TH

The Committee of five reported the following Apportionment of Representation in first Branch of Legislature for first Meeting consisting of 56 Viz.

p. 77

New Hampshire..	2	Deleware	1
Massachusetts ...	7	Maryland	4
Rhode Island	1	Pennsylvania	8
Connecticut	4	Virginia	9
New York	5	North Carolina ..	5
New Iersey	3	South Carolina ..	5
		Georgia	2

The Rule of Adjustment was required to be explained—It was answered it was a combined Ratio of Numbers and Property. This was postponed to take up the subsequent Part of Report in these Words—

---

[184] M. and the Journal are somewhat confused as to when this vote took place. M. originally had it on July 7, but eventually changed it to July 6. L.'s record shows that M.'s first impression was correct.

"But as the present Situation of the States may
"probably alter as well in point of Wealth as in the
"Number of Inhabitants[185] that the Legislature be
"authorized from Time to Time to augment the
"Number of Representatives and in Case any of the
"States shall hereafter be divided or any two or
"more States united or any new States created within
p. 78 "the Limits of the United States the Legislature shall
"possess Authority to regulate the Number of Repre-
"sentatives in any of the foregoing Cases upon the
"Principles of their Wealth and Number of In-
"habitants."

Question—9 Ayes—2 Noes—New York No.

It was then moved to refer the Apportionment
of Representation to a Committee of 11.[186]—a Member from each State.

Agreed to and Committee appointed accordingly.

Adjourned till to Morrow.[187]

---

[185] M. and Journal "their inhabitants."

[186] L. first wrote "13", then substituted "11".

[187] Lansing's record ends here, although he and Yates attended
the Convention the next day (July 10), as is shown by the record
of votes (Farrand I, 564, 570). They were not present after
July 10.

APPENDIX I, VOL. I

REPORT OF THE COMMITTEE
OF THE WHOLE

p. 49   1. Resolved that *it is the Opinion of this Com-*
the

mittee that *a national* Government of the United
States[1] ought to *be established* consis*ting* of a Supreme Legislative Iudiciary and Executive.[2]

2. Resolved that the national Legislature ought
to consist of two Branches.

3. Resolved that the Members of the first Branch
of the national Legislature ought to be elected by the
People of the several States for the Term of three
Years to receive fixed Stipends by which they may
be compensated for the Devotion of their Time to
public Service—to be paid out of the national Treasury to be ineligible to any Office established by a
particular State, or under the Authority of the united

p. 50   States (except those peculiarly belonging to the Functions of the first Branch) during the Term of Service
and under the national Government for the Space of
one Year after its Expiration.

4*th.* Resolved That the Members of the second
Branch of the national Legislature ought to be chosen
by the individual Legislatures to be of the Age of
thirty Years at least: to hold their Offices for a

[1] "of the United States inserted," after a vote on June 20, see
note 2.

[2] The italicized words were struck out as a result of a vote
on June 20. The Convention wanted to eliminate the irritating
word "national".

Term sufficient to ensure their Independency namely seven Years: to receive fixed Stipends by which they may be compensated for the Devotion of their Time to public Service to be paid out of the national Treasury: to be ineligible to any Office established by a particular State or under the Authority of the p. 51 United States (except those peculiarly belonging to the Functions of the second Branch) during the Term of Service and under the national Government for the Space of one Year after its Expiration.

5*th*. Resolved, that each Branch ought to possess the Right of originating Acts.

6*th*. Resolved, that the national Legislature ought to be empowered to enjoy the Legislative Rights vested in Congress by the Confederation, and moreover to legislate in all Cases to which the seperate States are incompetent, or in which the Harmony of the United States may be interrupted by the exercise of individual Legislation: to negative *all* p. 52 *Laws* passed by the several States contravening in the Opinion of the national Legislature the Articles of Union or any Treaties subsisting under the Authority of the Union.

7*th*. Resolved that the Right[3] of Suffrage in the first Branch of the national Legislature ought not to be according to the Rule established in the Articles of Confederation, but according to some equitable Ratio of Representation namely *in proportion of*[4] *the whole Number* of white and other free Citizens and Inhabitants of every Age, Sex and Condition including those bound to Servitude for a Term of Years and three fifths of all other Persons not comprehended

[3] M. "rights". The Journal agrees with L.
[4] M. and Journal "to"

in the foregoing Description except Indians not paying Taxes in each State.

p. 53   8*th*. Resolved that the Right of Suffrage in the second Branch of the national Legislature ought to be according to the Rule established for the first.

9*th*. Resolved that a national Executive be instituted to consist of a single Person to be chosen by the national Legislature for the Term of seven Years, with Power to carry into Execution the national Laws: to appoint to Offices in Cases not otherwise provided for: to be ineligible a second Time, and to be removeable on Impeachment and Conviction of mal-practice or Neglect of Duty: to receive a fixed Stipend by which he may be compensated for the Devotion of his Time to public Service to be paid

p. 54 out of the national Treasury.

10*th*. Resolved—that the national Executive shall have a Right to negative any Legislative Act which shall not be afterwards past unless by two third Parts[5] of each Branch of the national Legislature.

11. Resolved that a national Iudiciary be established to consist of one supreme Tribunal: the Iudges of which to be appointed by the second Branch of the national Legislature: to hold their Offices during good Behaviour and to receive punctually at stated Times a fixed Compensation for their Services in which no Encrease or Diminution shall be made so as to affect the Persons actually in Office at the Time of such Encrease or Diminution.

p. 55   12*th*. Resolved, that the national Legislature be empowered to appoint inferior Tribunals.

[5] M. omits "parts". The Journal agrees with L.

13*th*. Resolved, that the Iurisdiction of the national Iudiciary shall extend to Cases which Respect the Collection of the national Revenue, Impeachments of any national Officers and Questions which involve the national Peace and Harmony.

14*th*. Resolved, that Provision ought to be made for the Admission of States lawfully arising within the Limits of the United States whether from a voluntary Iunction of Government or Territory or otherwise with the Consent of a Number of Voices in the national Legislature less than the Whole.

p. 56   15*th*. Resolved that Provision ought to be made for the Continuance of Congress and their Authorities and Priviledges[6] until a given Day after the Reform of the Articles of Union shall be adopted, and for the Completion of all their Engagements.

16*th*. Resolved that a Republican Constitution and its existing Laws ought to be guarenteed to each State by the United States.

17. Resolved that Provision ought to be made for the Amendment of the Articles of the Union whensoever it shall seem necessary.

18. Resolved that the Legislative, Executive and Iudiciary Powers within the several States ought to be bound by Oath to support the Articles of Union.

p. 57   19*th*. Resolved that the Amendments which shall be offered to the Confederation by the Convention ought at a proper Time or Times after the Approbation of Congress to be submitted to an Assembly or Assemblies of Representatives[7] recommended by the several Legislatures to be expressly chosen by the People to consider and decide thereon.

---

[6] The Journal omits "and priviledges". M. agrees with L.
[7] M. omits "of representatives". The Journal agrees with L.

APPENDIX II, VOL. I

THE VIRGINIA PLAN, WITH AMENDMENTS MADE BY THE COMMITTEE OF THE WHOLE

p. 58   May 30, 1787. Copy of Resolves proposed by the Members of Virginia.

Mr. Randolph.

a.   1st. Resolved that the Articles of Confederation ought to be so corrected and enlarged as to

b. accomplish the Objects proposed by their Institution namely common Defence Security of Liberty and general Welfare.

2ndly. Resolved therefore that the Rights of Suffrage in the national Legislature ought to be pro-

c. portioned to the Quotas of Contribution or to the Number of free Inhabitants as the one or other Rule may seem best in different Cases.

3rdly. Resolved that the national Legislature ought to consist of two Branches.

4thly. Resolved that the Members of the

e. first Branch of the national Legislature ought

p. 59 to be elected by the People of the several States[8] for the Term of three Years[9] *to be of the Age of Years at least,*[10] to receive fixed[11] Stipends by which they may be compensated for the Devotion of their

---

[8] M. inserts "every . . ."

[9] The length of the term was left blank in the original resolutions; L. filled it in later as a result of a vote on June 12, see p. 49.

[10] The words in italics were struck out in Committee of the Whole on June 12, see p. 49, and have a line drawn through them here.

[11] L. first wrote "liberal", then substituted "fixed", as the result of a vote in Committee of the Whole on June 12, see p. 49.

Time in public Service—to be ineligible to any Office established by a particular State[12] under the Authority of the united States (except those peculiarly belonging to the Functions of the first Branch) during the Time[13] of Service and for the Space of one Year[14] after its Expiration — / to be incapable of Re-election for the Space of   after the Expiration of the Term of Service and to be subject to recal.[15]

p. 60   5th. Resolved that the Members of the second Branch of the national Legislature ought to be elected by those of the first out of the[16] proper Number of Persons nominated by the individual Legislatures— to be of[17] Age of   Years at least, to hold their Offices for a Term sufficient to insure their Independency, to receive liberal Stipends by which they may be compensated for the Devotion of their Time to the public Service—to be ineligible to any Office established by a particular State or under the Authority of the united States (except those peculiarly belonging to the Functions of the second Branch) during the Term of Service and for the Space of the Expiration[18] thereof.

p. 61   6th. Resolved that each Branch ought to possess the Right of originating Acts; that the national Legislature ought to be empowered to enjoy the Legislative Rights vested in Congress by the Confeder-

---

[12] M. inserts "or", which is certainly right.

[13] M. "Term".

[14] Blank in the original, and filled in later by L. as a result of a vote on June 12, see p. 49.

[15] L. marked off this last clause, since it was struck out by vote on June 12, see p. 50.

[16] M. "a".

[17] M. inserts "the".

[18] This has been garbled by L. In M. it reads "and for the space of   after the expiration thereof."

ation and moreover to legislate in all Cases to which
the seperate States are incompetent or in which the
Harmony of the united States may be interrupted by
the Exercise of individual Legislatures: to negative
all Laws passed by the several States *contravening
in the Opinion of the national Legislature the Articles
of the Union* and —— to call forth the Force of
the Union against any Member of the Union failing
to fulfil its Duty under the Articles thereof.[19]

    7thly. Resolved that a national Executive be
instituted to be chosen by the national Legislature for
p. 62 the Term of seven Years[20] to receive punctually at
stated Times a fixed Compensation for the Services
rendered in which no Encrease or Diminution shall
be made so as to affect the Magistracy existing at
the Time of Encrease or Diminution and to be ineligible a second Time *and removeable on Impeachment and Conviction for mal-conduct or Neglect in
the Execution of the Duties of his Office,*[21] and that
besides a general Authority to execute the national
Laws it ought to enjoy the executive Rights vested
in Congress by the Confederation and to appoint all
Officers not otherwise provided for.[22]

    8th. Resolved that the executive and a conven-
ient Number of the national Iudiciary ought to com-

    [19] This version of the sixth resolution agrees with M. Other
copies insert after "articles of the union" the words "or any
treaty subsisting under the authority of the union." See Farrand,
III, 593.

    [20] "seven years" inserted by L. as a result of a vote on June
1, see p. 28.

    [21] The italicized words were inserted by L. after they had
been adopted by the Committee of the Whole on June 2. See
p. 30.

    [22] "to appoint all Officers", etc., added by L. as a result of a
vote on June 1. See Journal and M.

p. 63 pose a Council of Revision with Authority to examine every Act of the national Legislature before it shall operate and every Act of a particular Legislature before a Negative thereon shall be final and that the dissent of the said Council shall amount to a Rejection unless the Act of the national Legislature be again passed or that of a particular Legislature be again negatived by ____ of the Members of each Branch.

9thly. Resolved that a national Iudiciary be established to consist of one or more Supreme Tribunals and of inferior Tribunals to be chosen *by the national Legislature*[23] to hold their Offices during good Behaviour and receive punctually at stated
p. 64 Times fixed Compensation for their Services in which no Encrease or Diminution shall be made so as to affect the Persons actually in Office at the Time of such Encrease or Diminution—that the Iurisdiction of the inferior Tribunals shall be to hear and determine in[24] the dernier Resort all Piracies and Felonies on the high Seas—Captures from an Enemy —Cases in which Foreigners or Citizens of the[25] States applying to such Iurisdictions may be interested or which respect the Collection of the national Income[26]—Impeachments of any national Officers and Questions which may involve the national Peace and Harmony.[27]

[23] Italicized words struck out by a vote on June 5, See p. 33.

[24] L. here omitted the words "in the first instance, and of the superior tribunal to hear and determine".

[25] M. "other States".

[26] M. "revenue".

[27] L.'s version of this resolution agrees substantially with M.'s; most other copies do not. L. gives new authority to show that inferior federal courts were planned in the first draft of the Virginia Plan, a view which has been contested. See Farrand, III, 593.

p. 65 10*thly.* Resolved that Provision ought to be made for the Admission of States lawfully arising within the Limits of the united States whether from a voluntary Iunction of Government and Territory or otherwise with the Consent of a Number of Voices in the national Legislature less than the whole.

11*thly.* Resolved that a Republican Government *and Territory of each State (except in the Instance of voluntary Iunction of*[28] *Territory)*[29] ought to be guarenteed by the United States to each State.

12*thly.* Resolved that Provision ought to be made for the Continuance of a[30] Congress and their Authorities and Priviledges until a given Day after

p. 66 the Reform of the Articles of Union shall be adopted and for the Completion of all their Engagements.

13*thly.* Resolved that Provision ought to be made for the Amendment of the Articles of Union whensoever it shall seem necessary and that the Assent of the national Legislature ought not to be required thereto.

14*th.* Resolved that the Legislative executive and judiciary Powers within the several States ought to be bound by Oath to support the *Articles of Union.*—national Government.[31]

15*th.* Resolved that the Amendments which shall be offered to the Confederation by the Con-

p. 67 vention ought at a proper Time or Times after the Approbation of Congress to be submitted to an Assembly or Assemblies of Representatives recommended by the several Legislatures to be expressly

---

[28] M. inserts "government and".

[29] The italicized words were struck out by vote on June 11, see p. 47.

[30] M. omits "a".

[31] According to M. "articles of Union" is the correct reading.

chosen by the People to consider and decide thereon.

The Consideration of the first Article being postponed the following were proposed.[32]

Q. 1. Resolved—That a Union of the States merely foederal will not accomplish the Objects proposed by the Articles of Confederation namely—

    Common Defence

    Security of Liberty and

    General Welfare.

2d. Resolved—That no Treaty or Treaties among any of the States as Sovereign will accomplish or secure their common Defence Liberty or Welfare.[33]

p. 68

3rdly. Resolved that a national Government ought to be established consisting of a supreme judicial Legislature and executive.

APPENDIX III, VOL. II

p. 80   IULY 5TH.—REPORT OF MR. GERRY.

The Committee to whom was refered the 8*th* Resolution reported[34] from the Committee of the whole House and so much of the 7*th* as hath[35] not been decided on submit the following Report—

That the subsequent Propositions be recom-

---

[32] This refers to the proceedings on May 30, when Randolph moved to postpone consideration of his first resolution to establish certain general principles, given below. See p. 24.

[33] This agrees with Y. M. has "no treaty or treaties among the whole or part of the States, as individual sovereignties, would be sufficient."

[34] M. "of the Report". Journal confirms L.

[35] M. "has". Journal agrees with L.

mended to the Convention on Condition that both shall be generally[36] adopted.

1*st*. That in the first Branch of the Legislature each of the States now in the Union[37] be allowed one Member for every 40,000 Inhabitants of the Description reported in the 7*th* Resolution of the Committee of the whole House—that each State not containing that Number shall be allowed one Member.

p. 81 That all Bills for raising or appropriating Money and for fixing the Salaries of the Officers of the Government of the United States shall originate in the first Branch of the Legislature and shall not be altered or amended by the second Branch and that no Money shall be drawn from the public Treasury but in pursuance of Appropriations to be originated by[38] the first Branch.

2*dly*. That in the second Branch of the Legislature[39] each State shall have an equal Vote.

APPENDIX IV, VOL. II

p. 83 COLONEL HAMILTON'S SYSTEM

1. The Supreme Legislative Power of the United States of America to be vested in two distinct[40] Bodies of Men, the one to be called the Assembly and[41] the other the Senate who together shall form

---

[36] L. first wrote "equally", then substituted "generally".
[37] M. "shall be". Journal agrees with L.
[38] M. "in". Journal agrees with L.
[39] M. omits "of the Legislature". Journal agrees with L.
[40] M. "different".
[41] M. omits "and".

the Legislature of the United States with Power to pass all Laws whatsoever subject to the Negative hereafter mentioned.

2. The Assembly to consist of Persons elected by the People to serve for three Years.

3. The Senate to consist of Persons elected to serve during good Behaviour—Their Election to be made by Electors chosen for that Purpose by the People—In order to this the States to be divided

p. 84 into Election Districts—On the Death Removal or Resignation of any Senator his Place to be filled out of the District from whence he came.

4*th*. The Supreme executive Authority of the United States to be vested in a Governor to be elected to serve during good Behaviour—The Election to be made by Electors—chosen by Electors,[42] chosen by the People in the Election Districts aforesaid—The Authorities and Functions[43] to be as follows—to have a Negative upon all Laws about to be passed and the Execution of all Laws passed—to have the entire[44] Direction of War when authorized or began— to have with the Advice and Approbation of the Senate the Power of making all Treaties—to have the

p. 85 sole Appointment of the Heads or chief Officers of the Departments of Finance War and foreign Affairs—to have the Nomination of all other Officers (Ambassadors to foreign Nations included) subject to the Approbation or Rejection of the Senate—to have the Power of pardoning all Offences *except*

---

[42] M. omits "chosen by electors". L.'s version is confirmed by Hamilton's own copy, and by Brearly and Paterson; see Farrand, III, 617.

[43] M. inserts "of the Executive".

[44] M. omits "entire".

Treason which he shall not pardon without the Approbation of the Senate.

5. On the Death, Resignation or Removal of the Governor his Authorities to be exercised by the President of the Senate till a Successor be appointed.

6. The Senate have[45] the sole Power of declaring War—the Power of advising and approving all Treaties—the Power of approving or rejecting all

p. 86 Appointments of Officers except the Heads or chiefs of the Departments of Finance[46] and foreign Affairs.

7. The Supreme judicial Authority of the United States[47] to be vested in   [48] Iudges to hold their Office[49] during good Behaviour with adequate and permanent Salaries—This Court to have original Iurisdiction in all Cases of Capture and an appellative Iurisdiction in all Cases[50] in which the Revenues of the general Government or the Citizens of foreign Nations are concerned.

8. The Legislatures of the United States to have Power to institute Courts in each State for the Determination of all Matters of general Concern.[51]

p. 87 9. The Governor Senators and all Officers of the United States to be liable to Impeachment for mal and corrupt Conduct and upon Conviction to be removed from Office and disqualified for holding

[45] M. "to have".

[46] M. inserts "War", which is the right reading, see article 4 above.

[47] M. omits "of the United States".

[48] Farrand, III, 618. In Hamilton's own copy the blank was filled in with "twelve". All others have the blank. Hamilton probably inserted "twelve" at a later date.

[49] M. "offices".

[50] M. "causes".

[51] Farrand, III, 618. Hamilton's copy defined the powers of these courts more closely, but all other copies agree with L.

any Place of Trust or Profit—All Impeachments to be tried by a Court to consist of the chief or senior Iudge[52] of the superior Court of Law of each State—provided that such Iudge shall hold his Place during good Behaviour and have a permanent Salary.

10. All Laws of[53] particular States contrary to the Constitution or Laws of the United States to be utterly void and the better to prevent such Laws being p. 88 passed the Governor or President of each State shall be appointed by the general Government and shall have a Negative upon the Laws about to be passed in the State of which he is Governor or President.

11. No State to have any Forces Land or naval and the Militia of all the States to be under the sole and exclusive Direction of the United States—the Officers of which to be appointed and commissioned by them.

[52] Farrand, III, 618. Hamilton's copy includes in this court the judges of the federal supreme court. No other authority includes them, and they were probably inserted in Hamilton's copy at a later date.

M. has "a court to consist of the Chief   or Judge of the superior court of law of each State"; Read has almost the same; Brearley and Paterson agree with L. The weight of authority seems to be on L.'s side.

[53] M. "the particular".

INDEX